Praise for *Overcoming Depressive Living Syndrome*

"This wonderful volume of hope will become a classic text for guiding people in developing a greater degree of joyful living—it's for anyone willing to accept the invitation and do the work. Earnie and Cara have succeeded in producing a readable and doable plan that will certainly be on my shelf to offer to clients as well as on my nightstand for my own continuing personal journey."

—Kathleen Burton, M.A.
Pastoral care counselor

"One of the finest books Earnie has written. He touches upon one of the most serious problems of our day, in theoretical and practical ways. He touches the core of the universal syndrome of loneliness and fear that afflicts our society. Congratulations, Earnie! I couldn't put it down!"

—James Kavanaugh
Author of
*God Lives: From Religious Fear
to Spiritual Freedom*

"I do not know a single person who does not have some symptoms of depressive living syndrome. Earnie has once again brought his singularly sharp analytical skills to bear on a modern-day plague. A desperately needed, superbly clear, and usable book."

—Janee Parnegg
Past president of the
National Episcopal Coalition
on Alcohol and Drugs;
1995 recipient of their prestigious
Samuel Shoemaker Award

"People with depressive living syndrome should rejoice simply in knowing that Earnie Larsen has tackled this difficult subject. He has identified the sources of the difficulty and established a process for overcoming it. In short, he has given new hope and a spirit of joy to all who will receive it."

–GUY LYNCH
Senior Minister, Church of Today
Warren, Michigan

"It was a joy and a renewed learning experience for me to review Earnie's new book on DLS. Every time I am involved with Earnie or his various publications, I find the information helpful for me personally and with other people in my life and my patients. In a primary-care office many people who come in have, at least as part of their complaint, symptoms that are based on the psychological stresses in their life.

"This book helps us understand where these thoughts come from, where our behaviors come from, how to examine them, how to learn from them, and how to change them. Probably the most important part of this book is the concept of change and the exercises that are outlined in helping one change, because if that isn't addressed, insight alone is not helpful. Life has the rainbows and the sunsets, but also the hurricanes and the tornadoes. They are always going to be a part of our lives, and the whole living process is a function of how well we grow and become healthier adults."

–ROBERT L. POWERS, M.D.
Clinical Professor of Family Practice
and Community Health
University of Minnesota

OVERCOMING DEPRESSIVE LIVING SYNDROME

How to ENJOY Life,
Not Just ENDURE It

OVERCOMING
DEPRESSIVE
LIVING
SYNDROME

Earnie Larsen

WITH CARA A. MACKEN

TRIUMPH
Liguori, Missouri

Published by Triumph
Liguori, Missouri
An Imprint of Liguori Publications

Library of Congress Cataloging-in-Publication Data

Larsen, Earnie.
  Overcoming depressive living syndrome : how to enjoy life, not just endure
it / Earnie Larsen, with Cara A. Macken.
     p. cm.
  Includes index.
  ISBN 0-89243-868-1 (pbk.)
  1. Depression, Mental—Popular works. 2. Anhedonia—Popular works.
3. Joy. 4. Happiness. 5. Self-help techniques. I. Macken, Cara A., 1969– .
II. Title.
RC537.L355   1996
616.85'27—dc20   95-46964

To my wife, Paula,
who amazingly has loved me
all these years.

Contents

A Note From the Authors

Although this work is co-authored, it is written in the first-person singular for simplicity and clarity. Most ideas, suggestions, and examples are the result of our mutual and collaborative efforts.

Introduction

Certain events have more power than others to teach us life's richest lessons. Like the burning bush for Moses, these special events call out with their wisdom in a way that can hardly be ignored or missed.

One such event for me occurred during a visit to England. While there, my wife and I had the opportunity to link up with a cousin of hers, an amateur historian and family genealogist. He took us to the ancestral church of my wife's family, where we visited the forgotten grave of her great-grandfather, a grave that dated from the early nineteenth century. The church itself dated back to Norman times.

The cemetery was full of graves of people who lived long before any Europeans had set foot on the soil of America. The touch of ghosts was everywhere. In those surroundings, I was repeatedly pierced by a single thought: *Sooner or later we will all lie in graves that hundreds of years later others will look at—as we are here. Those onlookers will not know who we were or that we had ever lived except for an aged and weather-beaten stone marker. The time will come when all that will remain of us is a memory. Then, with time, even that will be gone, for no one will remain who re-members us.* What became burning-bush clear to me as I stood there surrounded by long-forgotten and never-known people was the question, "Ah, but did you enjoy your life?"

Sooner or later we will all pass the way of those resting quietly in that ancient English cemetery. When we reach that passing, how will we reflect on our own individual lives? For all the reasons we might have had to moan and groan, regardless of all the ups and downs life held, despite the terribly pressing matters that crowded our serenity, did we enjoy life? Did we allow life to be a celebration, or was it more of an endurance marathon? Did we learn to smell the roses, or were we too busy going in the opposite direction—until it was too late? Of all the massive energies we spent across the span of our lifetime, did we have the foresight and wisdom to spend as much energy enjoying life as we did chasing shadows that vanished? Did we take the time and spend the effort to *learn* this greatest of all skills: the ability to enjoy life?

Standing at that old, unkempt grave of a man once dearly loved and busy about many things, I asked myself, *Am I enjoying life? Am I fashioning well the gift I give back to God, a life well and joyfully lived?*

What are the obstacles to a life "well and joyfully lived"? Why don't we live more joyfully? What stands in the way? For every reason we can concoct to justify less than joyful living, there are far more—and better—reasons to live with joy. Living our life "for others," for example, is not a justification for depressive living if it leaves no time or consideration to enjoy life ourselves. There is no virtue to a life lived in drudgery, no matter how the energy is spent. Surely one of the greatest gifts we give to others is a joyful hope in the goodness of life.

What then gets in the way?

Certain terms or labels naming the process that steals joy from living have filtered into common usage. "Codependency," "dysfunctional family systems," "adult-child syndrome," "abused inner child," and "shame-based living" are but a few. We can enter prolong arguments over the practical and clinical meanings of these terms, but their impact is clear: loss of joy. However we understand the origin and meaning of these terms, they all mean virtually the same thing: an inner process is established that generates fear, anger, and grief, which in turn limits healthy intimacy, satisfying relationships, and positive spirituality. Whatever these terms mean, their "fingerprints" are clear: a burdened heart and a life that is less than it might be. In the day-to-day experience of such a life, the face of God becomes less clear, the voice of God becomes muted. We find it more and more difficult to touch the heart of others or to allow our own heart to be warmed. This lingering fingerprint is "depressive living syndrome."

For some of us, this syndrome underlies full-blown clinical depression. Some of us realize it in any number of addictions, obsessive-compulsive behaviors, anxiety, or panic attacks. To be sure, other factors impact these very real living problems. At the core of them, however, is the influence of the "negative E-mail" we outline in this book.

Whatever else must be done to right a life gone crooked, depressive living syndrome—a deeply ingrained, wounded manner of viewing self, others, and life—must be addressed. Even when we right all the broken and unsatisfactory parts of life, this fingerprint remains. Even when medications have quieted violent, inner, emotional storms, and evened out wildly fluctuating mood swings, fundamental healing remains to be done. The problem is the fundamental pattern of what we've learned is "I." When that "I" is less than a joy-inspiring being, we must—and can—learn something else, if we're willing to spend the time and effort.

Does any of this sound familiar to you? Even if your life is free of clinical depression, addiction, or obsessive-compulsive patterns, is it all it might be? Although no life is perfect, can you learn to experience more joy? Before your name is weather-worn on a marker centuries from now, can you learn to laugh more, weep less, let go of what bogs you down, hug those whose presence is sacrament, sing the songs that are in your heart? Can you live so that when the ride is over, you can contentedly sigh, "Wasn't that grand"?

In these pages we thoroughly outline what this process of depressive living syndrome is, what it is made of, and how it works. We assist you in your own personal assessment by providing objective criteria and self-directed tools by which you might determine your own life satisfaction quotient. The chapter titled "The Problem Behind the Problem: The Big Empty" explores the connections between depressive living syndrome and the cause of that syndrome buried within the heart of the individual—the heart that, for all of us, is made for love.

Finally, we provide ample material on "What do I do now?" After all, it does little good to illustrate a problem without offering suggestions or directives that can lead to resolutions. In particular, goal-setting becomes a potent steppingstone to reversing the damage of depressive living. And because all of life is a returning to God, we focus on healing the wounded heart, *allowing* being the operative word. For it is never that God is unwilling with regard to our healing process; rather, it is we who do not *allow* the touch that heals.

It can be done. We need not live our days under the tyranny of depressive living. We have a choice.

I return in my mind's eye to that quiet graveyard. With all the sensitivity I can muster, I listen with an inner ear to whatever wisdom is lingering around that hallowed spot. Through all my busyness, all my major concerns, all my fussing and rushing about, I filter what I hear. And what is that? I hear a soft, silvery voice telling me that life is short, that my major concerns are mostly dust, and that the question, "Ah, but did you enjoy the ride?" is all that counts. It becomes clear: life is short; what we make of it is what we *can* make of it; and what we can make of it is considerable.

With every good wish, and with memories of the cemetery at Wooten Basset England, before a grave marker dated 1786…

EARNIE LARSEN

1

What Is Depressive Living Syndrome?

Are you happy? Is your life satisfying? Has your life been what you expected, at least for the most part? No one has a *perfect* life, of course; to hold up perfection as a standard is a sure way to make yourself miserable. But if the end were to come tomorrow, would you be able to say, "I'm glad I was here. It's been a good ride"?

Personally, I cannot think of a more important question. The topic is hardly idle speculation for a boring afternoon. It's not a bit like wondering about what is on the other side of a black hole in space. Rather, the question of personal satisfaction with life addresses a core issue for all of us. Regardless of our "accomplishments" and "victories," no amount of "success" makes up for a lack of personal satisfaction and fulfillment.

I'm not referring to rank selfishness. I'm not insisting that the entire meaning of life revolves around whether or not *you* are happy. Rather, I make the observation that many worthy and accomplished people are driven, unhappy, and morose–while others, who seem to have accomplished far less, move through life with a smile on their lips and a song in their hearts.

But the "success" our society values so highly is not the same as "Did you enjoy the ride?" or "Are you enjoying the ride?" In other words, is there a priority place in your life for love and happiness, for trust and an open hand that does not hold a hidden price tag? Is there time for family and friends? Do you laugh much? In a nutshell, are you *living* the classic advice we see in all those little books of wisdom that are so popular these days? Every one of those wise quotations, some going back thousands of years, speaks of the necessity of love and friendship in our lives.

If your life were near its end, what would you list among your deepest regrets and lost dreams? Are you living in such a way that your regrets are minimized and your dreams are fulfilled? Think about it.

Where All Paths Intersect

This book is not only about treating depression–whether that depression be full-blown clinical depression in any of its many and various degrees or its milder more temporary form, dysthymia. What is offered here will help anyone caught in the process–mental, emotional, physical, and spiritual–that underlies all these labels.

This book is not only about dealing with recovery from addictions or obsessive-compulsive behaviors in their many forms–although people who suffer with these issues may well be the same folks who are deep in depression. Depression often co-

coons addictions and obsessive-compulsive behavior. That is to say that those persons recovering from addiction or obsessive-compulsive behavior may well experience depression. After all, the addiction was used as a means of avoiding pain; once the addiction is removed, the pain, with all the guilt and fear that accompany such unshielded confrontation with life, must be dealt with.

This book is not only about facing all those terribly irritating and potentially dangerous traits that fall under the various titles of codependency, shame, adult-child syndrome, dysfunctional behavior, or common low self-esteem—although people dealing with some form of depression are often dealing with these issues as well. There are, however, millions who relate to the symptoms trumpeted in all the self-help books about codependency in any of its costumes, but who are not addicted or necessarily "depressed." The ideas here will be helpful to them whether they see themselves categorically or not.

This book is not only about those who have experienced disaster, with all the lingering trauma that follows. There are, of course, aftershocks when a loved one suddenly dies or there is betrayal in a primary relationship or you have been told of the presence of a terminal illness in your body. The guidelines that follow will certainly help break the power of such aftershocks.

This book *is* about the single point at which all these paths intersect—where they overlap, run together, mingle, and mix. Whatever the various starting points, whatever the differences, all these paths eventually come together to create a condition that strangles joy. Underlying and permeating all these roads, to varying degrees, is a pattern or process that encases the heart in concrete, making life more of an endurance contest than a celebration: this is depressive living syndrome.

Everything Is Related

Many of us feel that we have been condemned, like the Greek mythical figure, Sisyphus, who was dealt a famous punishment by the gods. Every morning, and all day long, he had the meaningless and useless task of pushing a mighty boulder up a hill–only to find it rolling down to the foot of the hill again in the evening. Like Sisyphus, many of us feel certain that we will be crushed by one huge rock or another–if not today, tomorrow for sure–regardless of what we try to do.

But life is not perfect. To expect it to be so is to set ourselves up for frustration and discouragement. To expect perfection, or just more than our share of contentment and satisfaction, is not wise. At the same time, it is neither wise nor sensible to settle for far less than is realistically possible. People who experience evident, constant joy and people who experience a prevailing joylessness are both in the grips of a negative process that is as deep as their fingerprints, as personal as the beating of their heart, as habitual and unnoticed as the very act of breathing.

A familiar athletic shoe advertisement tells us to "Just do it!" But all of us are "just doing it" every moment of every day. The question is *"What* are we doing?" What are we creating out of that inner mechanism that defines the reality we experience as our lives? This process is, of course, complex, yet relatively simple all the same. It is related to the way we think, yet, it's more than that.

All things are related. How we think is caused by and supported by how we feel–and how we feel is dictated by our reality. Yet this syndrome is more closely related to the *behaviors* that create our lives. And behavior does not exist in a vacuum any more than thoughts or feelings exist in a vacuum. Vacuums do not exist in human beings. Rather everything mixes, mingles, and prods at everything else, pointing the whole in a certain direction.

Like instantaneous E-mail, to use a technological analogy, the electrochemical information highway inside each of us is buzzing night and day. The "world" as we know it is not dictated by circumstances nearly so much as by the inner machinery we use to translate those outside circumstances. That inner mechanism is the culmination and the interaction—either positive or negative—of many forces existing within and around us, one force being fed by and feeding into another. We all stand on the shoulders of what and who went before us.

Our Western world, unfortunately, loves the straight line. We love logic and predictable conclusions. Capitalism is based on such a love affair; after all, how can we make a profit if we don't keep our eyes on the numbers? Numbers become the ultimate truth—or at least the only truth that really matters. So we create logical models. We tend to kick out of the picture that which doesn't fit into those models, no matter how true, relevant, or humane. If it doesn't fit, it doesn't exist.

In reality, however—at least a different reality—the true universal form is the circle. Everything is related. Everything is both cause and consequence, result and reason. Kick a rock on earth, and the effects, however faint, are felt on the furthest rim of the universe.

To think in this manner is to think relationally, but the Western mind has a hard time thinking relationally. We fixate on what *is* with such little thought to what we are setting into motion that will, in its turn, be a new *is* at some later date—and by then it may be too late. If we have learned anything from the focus on ecology, we should have learned that we all drink from the same well. But where will we drink tomorrow if we poison the well today?

In humans, this circular or cyclical think-feel-act process creates the behavior that creates the consequences we experience. This then steps up expectations and perceptions that E-mail the information to create similar, repeated thoughts-feelings-actions. If the direction of all that "information" is positive, then the quality of life will be predominately positive. Acorns grow oaks; oaks are grown-up acorns.

Let me give you a small but telling personal example. I live in Minnesota. One bitter-cold Friday afternoon, the wind chill fell to a brisk thirty-below. Everyone was in a hurry to get home after a long week's work, not to mention simply to get out of the cold. As we might expect, people were a bit short-tempered and somewhat crabby.

I stopped at a deli to buy some hot soup for dinner. The line was long, and the customers, normally pleasant, were impatient. The cashier, a young woman in her twenties, was the target of much hostile attention. The crowd's every move seemed so say, *Get going! Hurry up!* Yet the young woman remained solidly positive through it all; the hurry-up stares and impatient swaying of waiting customers did not melt her pleasant demeanor. She never seemed rushed and managed a cheerful word for everyone, whether they appreciated it or not.

When it was my turn to be waited on, the woman smiled and said, "Hot soup. How nice. That should taste really good on an evening like this."

That alone impressed me. Had I been in her place, I don't think I would have maintained such a positive stance. Then she took the time to wrap my soup in a second insulated bag. "This should help keep it warm until you get home," she said. Under the barrage of negative looks from the customers behind me, I asked the woman if she was always so chipper or if she had to work at it. "No, I don't work at it. It's just the way I am. Seems a better way to be to me."

I couldn't argue her logic, but I certainly marveled at her good fortune. Talk about being blessed! Apparently the process inside her inner space—all that frantic E-mail zapping around, plus the combination of genetic makeup, brain chemistry, and perhaps modeling from those in her family—left her with a treasure beyond price: a naturally positive outlook on life. I don't see many who are so blessed.

For many people, that inner process has turned negative: the glass is always half empty, life is never safe, and behind every smile is a hidden agenda. For these people, all human interaction is overlaid with fear, anger, guilt, and shame, and their lives are much less enjoyable than they might be. These people, of course, may or may not fit the category of severe depression or dysthymia; they may or may not be fighting the battle of recovery from addiction and compulsion; they may or may not have suffered severe trauma in their lives. But inside them all, this sour, grinding process is at work.

Complex in nature, this negative process creates negative consequences as surely as a bent-up cookie cutter produces misshapen cookies. Such people may have accomplished great works or nothing, done much good for others or never contributed a thing. But if their inner workings are motivated more by a sense of fleeing some deeply buried demon than moving toward freedom, they have not succeeded at life, regardless of any outstanding accomplishments. They have missed the bus. This is the depressive living syndrome cycle.

I offer another small example. A friend recalled an incident from his childhood that demonstrates the power of his negative E-mail that was set up some forty years ago when he was growing up in a seriously abusive family system. As a child, my friend could never get approval or even a smile from his terribly unhappy father. "I was just like a stump," he said. "I was just *there*. No one ever took notice of me."

He remembers going into town with his father one afternoon, to run errands and to go to the barber shop. At the time, haircuts were thirty-five cents. As an eight-year-old child, my friend was not getting a haircut; his hair was cut at home. Only his father got the "city cut." When the barber finished cutting his father's hair, however, he innocently turned to the young boy and said, "Okay, Kid, it's your turn. Hop up here. We'll get you cut in a second."

The child was horrified. He felt caught between a rock and a hard place. He was excited about getting a *real* haircut, but nervous about costing his father money. He didn't know what to do. As he timidly climbed into the barber's chair, he listened for his father's voice–but his father said nothing. His father's anger and discomfort were obvious, however. "My father didn't want to embarrass himself by saying anything," my friend said of this old and painful memory.

Today, forty years later, my friend clearly recalls his feelings of guilt. "I'm doing something wrong; I've become a nuisance because I'm getting something for myself." This episode, of course, engendered a batch of furious, frantic E-mail. But since he was already eight years old, my friend's E-mail patterns were strongly in place–so the message simply was being reinforced, a message that would fashion his reality for years to come.

I couldn't help but think of the striking difference between this lovely, kind man, so beset by demons, and the young check-out girl at the deli. Both good and worthy human beings, yet the content of their E-mail is as different as night and day.

In his adult years, my friend has worked hard to become a wealthy man. His many businesses all flourish. But is he happy? free? He told me another story about a lady friend of his (not a "serious" friend; he has never been able to sustain a serious, intimate relationship) who invited him to high tea at a ritzy hotel, followed by a stage show. Although the invitation sparked all the negative, ingrained E-mail messages, my friend focused on his desire to enjoy life before it was too late; he accepted the invitation.

How do you think the outing went? My friend's comments tell the story. "For some reason," he said, "I felt terribly uncomfortable at tea. I felt like I was doing something wrong, just sitting there doing nothing, spending money on extras." The familiar old guilt was upon him. "I felt like my father or some other authority figure was going to come in at any minute and drag me out by the scruff of my neck and tell me to get to work." Through the whole experience, my friend was in constant battle with his right to be there. Where had he gotten permission to spend as much time and money as he wanted? to go to a musical show and *enjoy* it, if he chose?

This man's life has been fraught with severe depression. He is a sober alcoholic who has been dry for some twenty years. Although he has helped countless others to this state of grace, his negative E-mail is still sent and delivered across his electrochemical information highway, reinforcing his stiff neck, tense shoulders, and lifelong loneliness.

There Is Hope

Perfect, life is not. But for how many of us could it be much better, much happier? Is there hope? If we find ourselves caught in a negative web of any making, is there realistic hope for change? Can the man in pain at the tea party ever develop a positive reality? Yes. There is always hope.

Consider this example. Another friend of mine, also a recovering alcoholic, also a graduate of the school of constant depression, told me that his E-mail (my term, not his) had served him up a terrifying case of agoraphobia, a close cousin to claustrophobia. This man had a tremendous fear of being closed in. Elevators, planes, the back seat of cars, would send him into uncontrollable panic. He was also a man who had realized great financial success. In every way, my friend *looked* like a winner, yet he had not been able to free himself of this pernicious trap. His negative E-mail was firmly in place.

After many attempts to overcome this joy-depriver, my friend founded a group for suffering agoraphobics. With unfailing love, support, and individual grit, his fellow sufferers struggled to reclaim their power of choice. Supporting my friend toward this end, the group decided on a collective effort. They would park a large, four-door car in the middle of a huge, empty parking lot and leave all the doors open. Then, with the love and support of the group standing nearby, and knowing he was making a free choice, my friend would climb into the back seat of the car. Slowly, with repeated efforts, he became comfortable.

Another sufferer, Peggy, was terrified not only of being in the back seat, but of driving at all. So, with the support of the group, Peggy and my friend worked together. My friend would sit in the back seat, and Peggy would sit in the front seat, behind the steering wheel. The car's engine would not be on; nothing would be moving. The two would just sit there. Thus powerful, positive new information was introduced into their E-mail circuits, affecting the thought-feeling-act process of both of them.

With time, by working through all the E-mail-produced fear and panic, my friend could tolerate others being in the car with him—and Peggy could put the key in the ignition. Eventually, by rearranging all the inner information that created so much of his outer reality, my friend actually allowed the doors of the car to be shut *with him in the middle* of a full back seat. And Peggy got to where she could start the car.

Still, the group would just sit there. It was all they could handle. The big car full of people sitting quietly, going nowhere—*outwardly* going nowhere. *Inside*, whole new creations were coming into being. Circuits were being rerouted, and new ones were being opened.

One landmark day Peggy turned the ignition and slowly steered the car around the parking lot. Someone asked, "Peggy, are you ready? Why not just drive out onto the frontage road? Let's go for a little ride."

Of course, Peggy was frantic. My friend said he experienced a tremendous sense of healing, however, when he leaned forward to encourage Peggy. At that moment, he cared more about Peggy's victory than his own fear. He did not *ignore* his fear; he did not focus on someone else to avoid doing his own work. Rather, he claimed and exercised his inner courage to deal with his own panic and twisted reality—and relief and freedom were his rewards. By practicing in the safe community of those who loved him, my friend arrived at a place where he could be a healer to another person, out of his own healing rather than denial.

Is there hope? Oh, yes. There is always hope—*if...*

Graced Moments

Most of our lives are graced, now and then, with brilliant moments of clarity. These moments, in the midst of the most ordinary events, reveal most extraordinary insights. Strange, these moments. They are like knives parting the dense veil of "the ordinary" to reveal a pearl of lustrous wisdom that somehow had never been noticed. Although the truth had always been there, only in that moment do we become aware of it—waiting there to be discovered.

A friend of mine recounted such a moment. He heard on a television newscast that it had been ten years since the *Challenger* spacecraft disaster. It was nothing more than a casual comment, but the fact struck him like lightning.

He said that in that instant, it became painfully clear to him that those ten years had gone by in a flash. He wondered how many ten-year stretches he had left. Yet in those years since the disaster, he had consistently mortgaged his happiness to the future in favor of "I'll kick back and enjoy life *when…*" When? When the next business deal comes through? when this or that legal mess gets cleared up? when finances are more secure? *When…*always *when.* But in that moment of clarity, my friend was graced with wisdom: he had no guarantee of the next ten days—let alone ten years. "It's as if that moment were written in blood," he said. "The message was clear: 'If you are ever going to get around to enjoying life, you had best get at it.'"

Such a graced moment of clarity occurred in own my life when my wife and I visited London, England, for the first time. It was lovely, absolutely lovely, yet everything was just slightly different: different money, different words, different driving habits. All those differences made us cautious.

A friend was letting us use her apartment while we were there. Of course, I didn't want to break anything; I didn't want to upset her belongings. Staying in someone else's house always makes me feel that way: like walking on eggs—someone else's eggs.

But one of the lamps in my friend's apartment didn't work. When my wife and I came in each evening, all the lights worked, except the one in the corner; it just wouldn't come on. As a result, one corner of the living room was left in darkness. Not being handy, and surely not wanting to break the lamp, I decided simply to leave it alone. My wife and I simply tolerated the dark corner. What difference did it really make, anyway? By and large, we got along fine. Just one dark corner; it didn't matter. We ignored it, walked around it. We just did without that part of the room.

Then in the last few days of our stay, another friend stopped by the apartment. He immediately noticed the dark corner. "Why don't you turn on that lamp?" he asked. "Why leave so much of the room in shadows?" I explained that I didn't know how to fix the lamp; that I didn't want to break someone else's furniture; and that a dark corner or two was really no trouble. It wasn't like we were stumbling around in total darkness. It was just that we were forgoing the benefit of a fully lit room.

The moment of clarity came to me in my friend's next comment. Looking at me like a wise old-timer spotting a green novice, he said, "Everything is connected to everything else. Everything has a cause. If you understand how a thing works, you can probably fix it." And with that, he proceeded to show me how to fix the lamp.

First, he tested the light bulb. After all, you don't have to be an electrician to figure out that if a lamp doesn't work, the light bulb might be burned out. He removed the bulb from the lamp in the corner and tried it in a lamp that worked. The light flared to life. The problem was not the bulb.

Next, my friend tried the outlet. If it wasn't the bulb, maybe no electricity was coming through. He asked if we had an appliance that we knew was working; we brought him a hair dryer. He plugged the hair dryer into the outlet—and it roared to life. It wasn't the outlet.

"Does the bulb in this lamp *never* work, or does it flicker?" he asked. "It's dead as a doornail," I said. "Never has worked at all."

"Then it's probably not a short. If the cord is shorted out, the lamp will flicker. What that leaves, nine times out of ten, is a blown fuse. This little box here on the cord is a miniature fuse box. I bet the fuse is out. Do you have a screwdriver?"

My wife and I looked at each other, blank as boards. "Nope," we said. "No screwdriver that we know of."

Again, with a wise look, my friend said, "You know, I bet there is a drawer in this flat somewhere that is full of knick-knacks, small tools, screws, and bolts. Don't you have a drawer like that back home?"

Indeed we did—and sure enough, after a quick snoop around, we found the drawer. In it we found a small screwdriver *and* a spare fuse. I thought of his words: "If you understand how something works, you can probably fix it."

With a replaced fuse, the light blazed to life; no more dark corners. There had been no good reason to tolerate all those shadows, to limit the amount of space in that room that was available to us. We put up with that dark corner because of a lack of understanding of how lamps work and a certain fear that resulted from that lack of understanding. Once we got past both of those limitations, reclaiming the room wasn't such a mysterious, immense, formidable task at all. As the man said, "Everything is connected to everything else." In wisdom language, that means "Don't let fear condemn you to the dark corners of life."

The Dark Corners Within

There are many kinds of dark corners. Some are in the outer space that surrounds us, and others exist in our inner space: in our minds, attitudes, and perceptions of ourselves.

In the same way that ignorance and fear led my wife and I to tolerate the dark corners of that London flat, many of us tolerate dark corners in our inner space, letting them diminish the quality of our lives.

So many of us seem to get much less from life than we bargained for! The glass is always half empty and no cloud has a silver lining. Why? Why do some of us manage to get so much *more* out of life, seeing the glass half full and a silver tinge to every cloud? When surrounded by both beauty and ugliness, success and failure, as we all are every day, why do some of us consistently opt for beauty and success while others, with equal motivation to choose either, consistently go with failure and ugliness? Why is that? Why do some of us live with dark corners and others fix the lamp and glory in the light?

On a recent television interview, I heard a movie star—surely one of the most beautiful women in the world—complain about her life. On the outside she had everything our society labels is important: fame, glamour, wealth, beauty. Yet she called her mansion a "pretty prison" where she is never left alone. Obviously, she suffers from seriously polluted inner space. Why? What is that inner space all about? Why are some people unhappy even when they *have* and seemingly *are* so much—and others, with far less, lead happier lives?

In contrast to this privileged "prisoner," consider a good friend of mine in her late sixties. Although she has very little money and is in poor health, she recently married again. About her new husband she says, "He has a large red birthmark on his face, but of course I don't even see it. His gentle soul is all I see." What causes the difference between my friend and the "successful" Hollywood personality?

Consider Robert, a fifty-ish ex-con, doing his best, but brimming over with repressed and exploding anger. One afternoon Robert and I decided to get together. While walking around a city park lake, we saw two men jogging very quickly toward us. Realizing that the walkway was not wide enough for the four of us, and sensing that Robert was becoming tense, I asked, "What are you going to do?"

"First, I'm going to bust that big one's jaw," he replied. "Then I'll take out the other one."

"Why do you want to do such violence when all we have to do is move a little to the side?"

Robert's answer reflected his E-mail history. "These runners in their fancy clothes think they're better than me. Well, people have been pushing me around all my life, and it isn't going to happen again." He had learned as a little boy, he said, that if you don't hit "them" first and hard, one of "them" will surely knock you silly.

"Life isn't fair," he said. "I never got a break in my life. So I take care of number one." (I am glad to report that I was able to talk Robert out of felonious assault on the lakeside.)

Now compare Robert to the world-famous physicist, Stephen Hawking, a man I was reading about on one of my endless plane trips. A renown author, Dr. Hawking is the world's preeminent authority on such arcane topics as black holes and the "space-time continuum" we read about in science fiction. Hawking cannot speak or move, except for a slight wiggle of his right thumb; he suffers with ALS (amyotrophic lateral sclerosis, also known as Lou Gehrig's disease).

The article highlighted Dr. Hawking's zest for life by recounting an incident at a convention of the brilliant and famous where he was a guest speaker (communicating with the aid of a portable computer). Because the conference concluded with a dinner dance, the convention hosts feared that the honored guest might take offense—or at least feel bad—if everyone danced while he remained chairbound.

Apparently, Dr. Hawking's inner space is as brilliant as his mind. At the conclusion of the dinner, when the dancing began, Dr. Hawking maneuvered his electric chair out onto the dance floor. By manipulating his right thumb on the joystick, he managed to move his chair back and forth, keeping with the beat of the music. If dancing was on the agenda, he would dance!

I can't help but place Robert and Dr. Hawking side by side. Of course, luck comes in many forms, but Robert bitterly complains *while walking and talking* about all the bad luck that has befallen him. He insists that he has no choices, and that life is unfair and ugly. Dr. Hawking, on the other hand, chairbound, drooling so uncontrollably that a full-time aide must constantly wipe his mouth, manages to propel his mind into the furthest heavens while his body—a broken cage—dances with the rest of the party!

The question isn't "Who is good and who is bad?" but "Why?" Why do some people live with dark corners and others set about creating light no matter what the circumstances? What is the process that chooses between the light and the dark? Humans are infinitely varied, of course; one size does not fit all. But is there anything that can be known and understood, so that when we're ready, we can "...fix what is broken"?

"Fixing," of course, is relative to the object that is broken or malfunctioning. Relative to life, therefore, what might "broken" or "malfunctioning" look like? Just knowing what we are supposed to accomplish in life can be confusing because everyone has an opinion. Society saturates us with our culture's opinion. As the T-shirts and posters say, "He who has the most toys when he dies, wins." Maybe.

But most of us know, in our moments of clarity, that the answer is not "possessions." And if there is more to life than possessions—*having* fame, *having* a slim, trim, healthy, and young body, *having* financial security—what is it? What is that *more*? Where does positive E-mail lead?

"Whom...Do You Deem Most Happy?"

While channel surfing through my cable options one evening, I came across a wonderful salesman shouting "Joy!" Part preacher, part positive-mental attitude guru, the man was all heat and fire. Sleeves rolled up, sweat rolling down his face, he shouted, "How about joy! Isn't that what we all want and yearn for—more joy in our lives?" He was entertaining in an inspirational sort of way—up to a point. "It's all a choice," he insisted. "A *simple* choice. We are absolutely as joyful as we allow ourselves to be..." Then he explained how his kit would enable the viewer to make that simple choice—for a modest price, of course.

Joy is a good word, isn't it. Although joy certainly has an aspect of choice, the choice often proves to be far from simple—or at least, it's not as easy as this evangelist-salesman indicated. Jesus uses the word *abundance* when he talks about joy: "I came

that [you] may have life, and have it abundantly" (John 10:10).
He speaks of the birds of the air and the lilies of the field that
neither plant nor spin, but are cared for by the Father. The key
to this abundant life, according to Jesus, is to draw so close to
the Father that there is no need for worry or fear.

Some five hundred years before Jesus (and no doubt five hundred years before that and five hundred years before that…) the
same issue was raised. In 440 B.C., the historian Herodatus was
invited to Athens to read from his writings on the history of the
war between Athens and Sparta. Such an invitation, it seems,
was the ancient equivalent of an author's tour.

Now Herodatus was born around 480 B.C.–far too late to have
any personal recollection of the great Persian War. Yet he made
a celebrity's life by writing an account of that bloody event, which
he simply called "History."

His "History" was not history as we moderns think of history.
It was not an exact account of dates and events, but a weaving of
popular belief and moral comments through the more or less
factual accounting of actual events. In his book, Herodatus told
the story of Croesus, son of Alyattes, King of Sardis, the richest
man in the world. To be "as rich as Croesus" meant to have as
much money as God.

In verse 30 of Book I, Herodatus tells of Solon, the great wise
man of Athens, coming for a visit. Solon actually lived some one
hundred years before Herodatus–but, remember, this is history
as the ancients perceived it. He says that Croesus had his ser-
vants show Solon his wealth, which took days:

> When [Solon] had seen them all, and, insofar as time
> allowed, inspected them, Croesus addressed this ques-
> tion to his distinguished visitor: "Stranger of Ath-

ens," he said, "we have heard much of your wisdom and of your travels. We know that you have visited many lands, from your love and knowledge and a wish to see the world. I am curious therefore to inquire of you, whom of all the men that you have seen, do you deem the most happy?"

Of course, Croesus expected this wise man, after seeing his vast wealth and being a guest under his roof, to tell him that he, Croesus, of all men on earth, was the happiest. But it didn't happen.

Solon, according to Herodatus, "without flattery, according to his true sentiment..." told the king that Tellus of Athens was the happiest. Well! Who was Tellus of Athens?

In answer to the frustrated king's question, the great sage of Athens explained that Tellus lived in a time when his country flourished. He had sons both beautiful and good, and each of those sons had equally beautiful and good children. And on top of that, he lived as he died, "...surpassingly glorious." In a battle between the Athenians and their neighbors, Tellus had come to the assistance of his countrymen, routed the enemy, and died on the field of battle. He was buried with full honors and the respect of his peers.

Not terribly impressed, Croesus grilled Solon further. "Who then after him do you deem the most happy?" Surely the richest man in the world would come in second at least! But not so.

Instead, Solon named two brothers, Celebes and Biton. Though not rich, Solon said, "...their fortune was sufficient for their wants." They simply were good sons. When their mother, wishing to attend a religious festival in honor of the goddess Hera at Argos, found that her oxen had wandered off, her mighty sons hitched themselves to her cart and pulled her all the way to the festival, where they immediately died of their efforts. For this great sacrifice, everyone at the festival honored both the sons and the mother who bore them.

After listening to this, Herodatus tells us, Croesus angrily cut Solon off:

> "What, Stranger of Athens, is our happiness, then?
> Is our happiness so utterly set at nought by you that
> you do not even put us on a level with private men?"

Solon's answer is twenty-five hundred years old, yet it rings with crystal clarity even today. The wisest man of Greece said:

> "For yourself, Croesus, I see that you are wonderfully
> rich, and are king over many men. But with respect
> to your question, I have no answer to give, until I
> have heard that you have closed your life happily. For
> assuredly, he who possesses a great store of riches is
> no nearer happiness than he who has only what suf-
> fices for his daily needs…unless it so happens that he
> continue in the enjoyment of all his goods until the
> end of life. He who unites the greatest number of
> advantages, and retaining them to the day of his death,
> then dies peacefully, that man alone, sire, in my opin-
> ion, is entitled to bear the name 'happy.'"

Drawing on a more recent example, I have a group of friends who are involved in a positive-thought way of life built on what they call "universal principles." It is a life system designed for increasing participation in whatever this greater dimension of life is called, what the Greeks called "happiness." One of their universal principles is called the "principle of abundance." This principle rests on the fact that life is so full of obtainable abundance that you actually have to work hard if you want to *reject* all of it.

But I wonder. If this is true, if we actually have to pound heavy four-by-fours over our door to keep abundance from overwhelming us, then a lot of us have learned to be very good carpenters—and the question remains: why? Why would we deny ourselves abundance if it is at hand, especially since we claim that we want this abundance so badly? With all due respect to my friends, the TV guru, and King Croesus, I suspect that, though the claiming of this abundance is indeed a choice, it is far from a simple choice. If it were easy and simple, we would all be transformed people.

The Magical, Mystical Machine

Inside each of us is an incredible network of neurons firing billions of times a second, creating the perceptions from which our reality is fashioned—a reality which then, in turn, further forms our perceptions. Millions upon millions of bits of information are constantly filtered down from the conscious mind to the subconscious, pulling the strings of reality as we see it. As this information comes filtering up again in a continuous feedback loop, it returns to the conscious mind in one form or another. Perhaps it is our "unreasonable" and "irrational" response of panic and anger at being "caught" in traffic, or being depressed at not being invited to some social function. Others don't seem angered, panicked, or depressed with these same set of circumstances. Why?

For some of us, this feedback loop into the conscious mind is affected by a terrible fear or defiance of authority. For some of us, it is affected by our inability to treat ourselves well; some of us find it impossible to treat ourselves as gently and courteously as we treat people we love—or even total strangers. For some of us, the thin but steellike back to all this data, filtered and forgotten but ever present in the subconscious, is affected by our drive to produce more, our tendency to worry about impending doom, or our need to continually prove ourselves.

The examples are endless. The process is common to all examples however: *we learned, we practiced, we became.* When this process occurs in a negative context, the result is depressive living syndrome (DLS).

DLS may not be full-blown depression; it may not be clinical depression at all (or it could be). The point is that this process, the result of this magical, mystical machine operating within all of us, retards joy. Life becomes less than what it can be, and the gift we give to God is diminished.

Life is not perfect. It never will be because it isn't meant to be. To seek perfection rather than growth is the downfall of many—and how well that feeds into certain versions of DLS.

If not perfect, however, can life be *made* better? Can we *make* our lives more joyful? Yes. Joylessness is not at the root of DLS; DLS is at the root of joylessness. DLS: the culmination of endless bits of negativity filtering into our subconscious and reemerging into our conscious life as deflectors of God's beauty and joy…and of our own tremendous possibilities.

2

The DLS Profile:
A Self-Assessment

In my experience of helping people cast light into their dark corners, the one comment I hear most often at the start of the journey is, "Oh, but you don't understand, I...." Fill in the blank for yourself: "...am German," "...am Irish," "...am Scandinavian," "...am the adult child of alcoholic parents," "...am the product of a home where love was never expressed," "...am from a poor socioeconomic background," "...was raised by strict Catholics (Protestants, Jews)," "...was raised with no religion at all."

Some of these "entry-level conditions" are, indeed, heartbreaking: "I was an incest victim." "I was abandoned as a child." "I never had a home." As painful and critical as these particular circumstances are, however, we are responsible for our own depressive living syndrome—or at least we are responsible for what happens from now on. For each person trapped in a negative web of conditioning, there are others, from the same negative web, who have fought their way out. We need not live forever in our dark corners. Not that freedom is an easy choice; not that great courage isn't needed. But the choice to change—at least to start changing—is ours. We first need to put aside our fear and understand what "needs to be fixed."

Take a good look at where you are right now; after all, it's pretty hard to get a fix on where you want to go if you don't know where you are. The following self-evaluation tools will help bring you closer to that understanding. They may help you better envision the role your history (roots) plays in fashioning the condition (fruit) of your life today. As in all life forms—human life included—there is a strong correlation between nurture and nature.

The first tool is a collection of life scenarios. Each scenario outlines the roots of an individual's life and the fruits that person realizes today. At the end of each scenario, you are invited to reflect on your own life experience and "rate" the degree to which you can identify with the details of that scenario.

The second tool is a more specific exercise that invites you into an "up close and personal look" at your life satisfaction quotient.

Life Scenarios

These scenarios are typical "life stories" as many of you experience them. The roots consist of the individual's history, and the fruit is the end product of the roots: what his or her life is like today.

Read each scenario carefully. After each one, indicate your identification with the situations represented: **1** means "I do not in any way relate to this scenario"; **10** means "This scenario strongly reflects an ongoing pattern in my life." As you will note in these scenarios, the day-to-day experience of life obviously determines the degree to which people enjoy their time on earth–not life in general, but *their own*–the only life (as far as any of us knows at this time) that they will ever live.

If an image other than roots and fruit is more comfortable for you, by all means use it. The important thing is to begin to think relationally! Nothing just *is*–all by itself and on its own. Everything that happens is *caused*. Remember: if there are dark corners in your living room, there are *reasons* why. And if you are going to chase the shadows away, you must understand how the lamp works and what you need to do to turn it on.

The most important outcome of this exercise is not simply your self-rating, but a developing recognition of the *relationship* between a life scenario and the resulting life satisfaction quotient.

Cynthia

Roots: As a child, Cynthia was told that she was a "big girl"; not fat; not obese; just "big." Perhaps these comments were meant to be kind; perhaps the comments simply referred to the fact that she was, indeed, a large girl; tall. In grade school, Cynthia was not only taller than all the boys in her class, but she also outweighed them. In high school, she reached the six-foot mark.

No doubt there were other girls who were "big," who were told they were "big," but who wore their size like a badge of honor. Cynthia, however, did not. To her, *big* meant "ugly." *Ugly* meant "freakish." *Freakish* meant "unacceptable." As a result, Cynthia became ashamed of her body, and people who are ashamed of their bodies are ashamed of themselves.

In all of us, of course, there's always more than one thing going on at any given time. Cynthia was not only "big"; she was also the girl born after a brother who was the family hero. This brother got attention and affirmation, while Cynthia simply was acknowledged as being "big."

Cynthia's family was on the lower end of the economic scale. Thus her clothes were far from stylish, and she stood out among the better-dressed children from middle- and upper-class families.

These factors and many more combined into a toxic stew. Cynthia never felt adequate. She never felt she quite measured up. Because her self-esteem was chronically low, she developed coping techniques, such as avoiding responsibility by pretending she didn't know what was going on. She learned to play dumb. And, of course, the more she played dumb, the more she was perceived as being dumb. And the more this perception spread and deepened, the more she was treated as a dim bulb.

Fruit: Today Cynthia seems to cope quite well. She has friends, plays sports, goes to parties. But inside, down where her thoughts are born, she never feels accepted or safe. All these factors have combined and express themselves in an eating disorder. This vignette is not *about* eating disorders, however. It is meant to point out the pressures that start to build when a person, in this case Cynthia, *perceives* herself or himself to be freakishly inadequate.

To what extent can you identify with this scenario?

1 – 2 – 3 – 4 – 5 – 6 – 7 – 8 – 9 – 10

Bill

Roots: Bill's father was a policeman from the rough-and-ready school. His idea of preparing his son for life was to make him tough, to teach him that he didn't need anyone and couldn't really count on anyone being there for him. Feelings were to be kept tightly in check. Pain and discomfort were not messages from the body saying, "Something is wrong; take care of me," but "This is a test—so prove how tough you are."

One of Bill's earliest memories of "failure" (in his father's eyes) was when his father enrolled him in a tiny-tots' boxing tournament sponsored by the police department. Bill was six years old. He didn't like to fight and really had no idea what boxing was all about. He wanted to play with other kids, not hit them.

Yet there he was, fitted out in huge gloves, standing inside a ring, everyone looking at him, and unsure of what was supposed to happen. His father was in his corner urging him to run across the ring and hit the other boy. When the bell rang and the other boy charged across the ring and hit Bill smack in the face, Bill was thoroughly confused. Why would this boy want to hit him?—and there was his father shouting at him to hit back.

Bill didn't want to hit anyone. He retreated to his corner, tears in his eyes, hoping his father would help him. He wanted his father to stop this frightening event, to acknowledge his pain, and to make this other boy go away.

Fruit: Bill is now thirty-eight years old and a dedicated, loving father. Yet he worries about his ability to be emotionally present to his son. With all his heart, he wants things to be different for his sons.

Haunting Bill's memory is his father hurling words at him like "coward" and "no-good son of mine." Bill doesn't remember how long the terrible boxing match lasted, but within his inner spaces, it continues to this day, decades later.

The boxing match is one event of hundreds that Bill can remember. Some of these events are much more graphic than others, but they all add up.

To what extent do you identify with this scenario?
1 – 2 – 3 – 4 – 5 – 6 – 7 – 8 – 9 – 10

Margo

Roots: Margo became a mother at ten—not in the physical sense, but in every other way. With an alcoholic father and a mother who coped with her difficult life by always "being sick," Margo was left to take care of herself and her two younger brothers and sister. More than any adult in the house, Margo took responsibility for laundry, housecleaning, cooking, and helping the younger children with their schoolwork. What little approval she received was focused on what she did, not who she was. Margo was "so grown up," "my little right-hand worker," "so wonderfully unselfish." Wanting approval as all humans do, Margo learned quickly how this most precious of all gifts was to be won: by working even harder at being superresponsible. Taking on impossible tasks came to feel normal to her. Sacrificing her needs and wishes for the needs and wishes of others became as natural to her as breathing. It felt right.

Fruit: Today Margo is becoming aware of the fact that she has a great deal of difficulty setting healthy boundaries around her own needs, and that she seems to surround herself with weak, needy people who are not able to give back to her. She is beginning to understand why she never has time for herself, or more to the point, why she feels she *doesn't have a right* to put herself first. What state of affairs could more surely damage one's ability to celebrate life?

To what extent do you identify with this scenario?
1 – 2 – 3 – 4 – 5 – 6 – 7 – 8 – 9 – 10

Greg

Roots: Many people in their twenties come from families of divorced parents. Not all of these people develop the seduction-rejection mode of managing relationships—but Greg did.

Greg's parents were divorced when he was thirteen. For reasons specific and unique to him, Greg can still recall the "vivid chill" of coming to grips with the fact that one of his parents was leaving.

Fruit: Greg does not understand his fear of commitment. At twenty-six, when many of his friends are married, Greg struggles with intimacy. Deep inside he knows that there is a line drawn in the sand of his soul, and no one is allowed to go beyond that line. When that line feels well guarded, he is charming, engaging, warm, and companionable. Anyone watching him with a lady friend would think for sure there were wedding bells in the future.

But invariably, when a relationship encroaches on that line, red flags wave all over the place. Fear flares up; panic mounts. For no reason he can name, Greg loses interest and begins to search for ways to end the relationship.

Being a good guy who hates conflict or even the idea of hurting anyone's feelings, Greg finds ending these relationships to be brutal. Exchanges drag on and on, the truth is never spoken, decisions are not made, disrespectful behaviors develop–behaviors that Greg would *never* be party to in a million years, until that mysterious line is approached. Most confusing of all to Greg (not to mention to his lady friends) is the fact that as soon as he sabotages the dangerous relationship, "all of a sudden" he is back in the mode of enticement; his lady friends call it a game. Inevitably, however, he arrives at that "line" and the back-off behavior starts all over again.

Greg loves his parents, although he went through a long period of being angry with both of them for "doing this to him." It was just *unthinkable* that this tragedy should befall him. It was one of those things–like starving to death or getting kidnapped–that only happened to other kids.

Greg says he will never forget the terror of wondering if his world would fall apart. Would he ever see his parents again? Would they hate each other? Would they come to see him play ball or graduate from school? Would they marry someone else and make him call a stranger "Mom" or "Dad"?

To what extent do you identify with this scenario?
1 – 2 – 3 – 4 – 5 – 6 – 7 – 8 – 9 – 10

Janet

Roots: Unlike Margo, who was constantly praised for achievement, Janet was told, verbally and nonverbally, that she should never set her goals too high. Around her house there was an unwritten rule that said just "getting by" was as much as anyone could ever hope for. Though she did well in school, Janet got the same message there that she got at home: when the prize at stake is something that really counts, let someone else go for it. Janet learned to assume that if it was important, she not only *wouldn't* understand, but was *incapable* of understanding.

Janet "learned" that she was not smart. She also learned that not being smart was okay because she was cute. That was her fast ball: looking good. For most of her life, Janet felt like an ornament. The message was: "Look good, but keep your mouth shut or they will *know!*"

Janet recalls a hot and heavy discussion—a shouting match—that blew up between her father and an aunt with whom she felt a close kinship during her teen years. For some reason, getting too close to this particular aunt was subtly discouraged. According to Janet's parents, this aunt was a "troublemaker." The heated war of words on this particular day was about women's rights before it was a movement; the aunt was championing women's rights.

Janet recalls her father's red face, the rage in his words, and the equal strength and vigor of her aunt's reaction. When finally the aunt left, Janet's mother quietly explained that, although everyone loved the aunt, she had strange ideas and shouldn't be taken too seriously.

Fruit: Although she could not verbalize it accurately for many years, today Janet knows what she was afraid *they* would *know* that nothing but empty space was behind her pretty face. After all, she was never encouraged to think, never asked her opinion. No one ever expressed respect for her insights. Slowly she came to believe that she *had* no insights and that her opinions could carry no weight.

Janet married a man just like her father. "My husband has yet to recognize anything really admirable about me—except how I look. Even though I have gone back to college and carry a 4.0 average, he still considers me hardly worthy of an important discussion. He treats me like a child, and I'm just beginning to understand how much I resent that."

To what extent do you identify with this scenario?
1 – 2 – 3 – 4 – 5 – 6 – 7 – 8 – 9 – 10

Jack

Roots: Jack's parents were people of their times. They were proper, hardworking, no-nonsense people. They were not abusive, but neither were they warm and affectionate. "Family" was simply the group of people into which you were born and with whom you lived. There was no touching in Jack's family, no hugging, no knee-sitting, no warm fuzzies of any kind. Wrestling around on the floor with his father was as improbable as going to church in your bathing suit. Never did Jack feel the delicious fun of a whisker burn in his father's embrace.

Work was the highest value in Jack's family, followed by proper decorum. When his mother passed away, Jack recalls vividly that his father never shed a tear. As somber as a stone wall, his father told him, "Stand tall and be a man—no tears. We come; we go. Such is life." Jack was taught that to be successful, you do whatever it takes, that successful people are simply those who are willing to do what others are not.

As a youngster, Jack was always willing to work on Saturdays and Sundays. As an adult, he tried to be a devoted parent, although he often missed occasions that were important to the kids because he was out of town or otherwise busy with work. He always figured that whatever he missed was offset by what his kids were able to do because of the financial success of his efforts. Besides, Jack never heard the kids complain when he needed to come across with money for summer camp, extra dance lessons, or the latest and best fashions.

Fruit: Today Jack is sixty-three, financially successful, a grandfather. As he enters the last third of his life, a new awareness creeps around the corners of his existence: "There must be something more to life than amassing wealth." Jack would never consider himself a greedy or materialistic man. He simply has spent most of his life creating an abundant, protective lifestyle for his family.

Jack's drive to build an empire has died down; he is no longer interested in accomplishments and security. Gradually, Jack is realizing that his treasure lies in connections with people—mostly his family. He would never have thought this possible a few years ago, but now he wants to love and be loved—that's all. He wants to belong, to be special to those he loves. He wants to make magic between himself and his grandchildren. When he sees television commercials featuring grandparents and their kids, he feels the same kind of urge, the same kind of "I want that," he used to feel when he saw advertisements for luxury cars or cruises.

There's one problem: Jack has no idea how to get what he wants. When he yearns to take his grandchildren in his arms, to bury his face in their sweet-smelling hair, to talk fairy-tale nonsense to them, to make jokes and share secrets, to hold their hands and tell them how precious they are to him, he doesn't know how. He isn't even sure what it is he doesn't know how to do. He does know that there is something missing in him, and in its place, there is an ache that no amount of money or material things will touch.

To what extent do you identify with this scenario?

1 – 2 – 3 – 4 – 5 – 6 – 7 – 8 – 9 – 10

Angie

Roots: Angie suspects that she was an incest victim, although specific details are difficult for her to recall. The sexual abuse, if it did occur, was not at the hands of her distant and uncaring father. Rather, she believes it happened with her godfather, her father's best friend.

When her parents were divorced, Angie's father moved to a distant state where he could be closer to his good friend: Angie's godfather. Every summer, in accordance with the court order, Angie would be shipped off to stay with her father. At some point during the summer, she would spend several days with her godfather. She suspects that the crimes against her were committed during these times.

Angie remembers trying to tell her father something about her godfather, something frightening and confusing and sexual. Her father's response was total rejection. He accused Angie of lying, blamed her for whatever might have happened, and refused to tolerate any further comments. So the cycle continued; Angie felt there was nothing more she could do. After her father died, Angie's out-of-state visits ended, of course, but Angie was left with a clear imperative: "Don't make waves; never accuse others of wrongdoing. If something wrong happens, you probably brought it on yourself and have no one to blame but yourself–besides, no one will believe anything you say to the contrary."

Angie learned that she was alone in finding a way to survive and make sense of the unimaginable. No matter how counterproductive or self-defeating her behavior might prove to be, she had to find ways to get around *her* problems. Taking all blame onto herself was an effective way of wringing sense from the flinty stone of nonsense.

Fruit: Today Angie perceives herself to be defective, spoiled, broken. She feels she is a second-class person who doesn't really qualify for a first-class mate.

Angie—like everyone else in these vignettes—is an unusually nice person. She functions well, holds down a job, and goes about her business much like everyone else. But Angie is *so* nice, *so* willing to please, *so* trusting of others, that she frequently finds herself in lose-lose situations, trying to make sense out of nonsense. She is terribly vulnerable to being taken advantage of by anyone who invites her to believe that whatever happens is her fault. There is no story so bizarre that she won't try to find some sense in it, even if it means taking blame onto herself—as long as others are not held responsible.

This cycle has led Angie through two marriages and two divorces. To a large degree, her life remains chaotic. Her second marriage was to a womanizer. She would never call him a sex addict, but as far as her experience of him went, he was incapable of fidelity. Whenever they were out—whether at a party, a movie, or just walking down the street—he would ogle every woman he saw. Flirting was his way of life. To him, women were not persons, but conquests.

This behavior, of course, deeply wounded Angie, who was the most loyal of partners. She simply could not understand why her husband would act that way. Because of Angie's trusting nature and her lack of ability to trust her own instincts, this toxic relationship dragged on much longer than it might have. Her philandering husband never owned the fact of his behavior. When

Angie complained too vigorously, his mode of operation was to blame *her*. He would accuse her of affairs, confront her about her flirtatious behavior, and rail at her about how deeply she embarrassed him.

True to form, Angie would then try to make sense of the nonsense. She would wonder if she was, in fact, flirting and didn't know she was. Maybe she *was* sending out come-on signals. Perhaps her husband's interest in other women was all in her imagination. Perhaps she was actually pushing him away with her suspicions. He often told her that no other man he knew would put up with such abuse. Perhaps it *really was* all her fault.

To what extent do you identify with this scenario?
1 – 2 – 3 – 4 – 5 – 6 – 7 – 8 – 9 – 10

Pauline

Roots: Pauline is adamant about loving her parents. She had a wonderful, loving home; no divorce, no alcoholism, and certainly no sexual abuse. Yet her own twenty-five-year marriage was characterized with abuse and disrespect—and she doesn't understand why. The pain she endured during the breakup of her marriage and the fear she now has about her own ability to make sane decisions in future relationships are utterly mystifying to her. As always, she says, she will just have to depend on Jesus.

Throughout her childhood, Pauline's family leaned on religion as their rock in the storm. Cruising through a crowded parking lot, the family simply asked the Lord to find a space. Facing medical situations, they asked God to minimize the pain. God could provide a date for the prom or good weather for a family outing.

Pauline and her family believed that they were puppets tethered to the hand of God. In their theology, God directly intervened in their lives thousands—perhaps millions—of times a day. Everything that happened was "God's will." They had better have God on their side—or more precisely, they had better stay on God's good side—or they were hopelessly lost. If they did wrong, God might just arrange for someone to break a leg, flunk a spelling test, or even lose a parent.

Pauline's family believed that keeping the rules kept one on God's good side. This became the end-all and be-all of life for Pauline: do not break the rules. Although she doesn't remember being taught this specific precept, she came to believe that since all rules came from God, all rules were to be obeyed with the same rigor. All rules were equally important, and breaking the rules was the same as sinning. Using bad language, cheating on a test, telling a lie, stealing a piece of candy: all were offenses (sins) that could put her or anyone on that shady, dangerous path toward tragedy (punishment).

Anyone in authority could communicate these rules; authority was God. Pauline didn't have to understood why a rule existed; she didn't have to respect the position of authority or the person in authority who issued and/or enforced the rule. If a rule was in place, it must be from God, and she had better obey if she didn't want "the will of God" to cause major grief for her or someone she loved.

Pauline heard, believed, and obeyed without question. At age twenty-two, Pauline married a military man who believed in the strength and power of authority, obedience, rules, and laws. He strongly believed that every relationship, every home, should be run military-style, complete with a superior and a subordinate. There had to be rules, and every rule had to be followed at all cost. The worst possible breach of ordered life would be to break the chain of command. His favorite saying, as Pauline recalls, was "You don't have to understand to obey."

Fruit: Today Pauline is forty-seven years old. Some would call the twenty-five years between Pauline's wedding and divorce a steady decline into godlessness. Others would call it a steady *incline* toward self-actualization.

Pauline was and is a smart, talented woman. As the years went by, the role of errant, witless child increasingly galled her. She had questions, good questions, questions that needed to be raised. As she was criticized for raising her questions, she began to see that there was something fundamentally flawed in a belief system that denied the questioning process. Yet her E-mail was entrenched; after paying the often humiliating price for each question ventured, Pauline would come face to face with the demon of guilt, the imperative to live out her old learned truths. It felt *right* to simply shut up and obey.

Gradually, Pauline's emerging belief about what was fair and "godly" pushed the marriage relationship beyond what it could bear. Soundly accused of being unfaithful and threatened with eternal hellfire, she now goes her own way. She doesn't know exactly who she is, but she does know that she is not a passive, intimidated, little mouse. She knows, too, that whoever she is now, she is becoming a free human being. Laughingly, she says that she feels like a person who has been frozen in ice for five thousand years. Like that person, she has thawed.

To what extent do you identify with this scenario?
1 – 2 – 3 – 4 – 5 – 6 – 7 – 8 – 9 – 10

To evaluate yourself, add the numbers you circled. If your total is **0–40**, you are most likely on solid ground; DLS is not a problem for you. If your total is **40–50**, the likelihood of DLS is moderate; you may want to consider seeking help and support. If your total is **50–70**, DLS is a very definite possibility; some fundamental changes are in order. If your total is **70–80**, severe DLS exists. Keep reading this book.

These eight brief scenarios are far from an exhaustive catalog of typical life stories. At a recent seminar, one of the participants pointed out that these scenarios are just people; they are everyone; they're like snatches of Psychology 101. Exactly. My intention is not to trot out exotic pathologies or grotesque perversions of human behavior. As commonplace as these scenarios may be, the underlying patterns they represent guarantee to diminish the degree of joy in our lives—and the less we live with joy, the more we live with DLS.

Life Satisfaction Quotient

To get "up close and personal," take a moment to determine your life satisfaction quotient: how satisfied you are with your life as a whole. On a scale of **1–10**, indicate how satisfied you are.

Before you make your self-evaluation, however, slow down. The common tendency is to not only rush an evaluation of this nature, but to put yourself where you think you *should* be. It's easy to get confused with guilt or toxic religion: "I am so blessed already that I don't have any right to think my life should be better." Some of us immediately revert back to "What about all the starving children in the world?" as a denial of our own misery.

Be aware of all the attitudes and perceptions that might prevent you from making a realistic evaluation. Fight off whatever conditioning urges you to select a score that does not truly reflect how you see your life. What is your truth?

$$1 - 2 - 3 - 4 - 5 - 6 - 7 - 8 - 9 - 10$$

A score of **0–3** indicates severe dissatisfaction. You probably see your life as totally unsatisfactory and are desperate for a change. A score of **3–5** indicates a high degree of dissatisfaction. Something is truly wrong, though exactly *what* might be a mystery. Your life is a constant source of disappointment and frustration. A score of **5–6** indicates that you believe life really should be more satisfying. You are not desperate, disappointed, or frustrated. Rather, you know, deep in those hidden places of yourself, that you are struggling far too much. Life should not be this hard. A score of **7–9** indicates that you believe life could be brighter. You know that nothing is perfect, of course, and that unrealistic expectations about how smooth life "should be" are a sure way to sabotage what happiness is available. But you're in touch with the fact that there is room for improvement, and you are willing to search for what you need to get all that the cup will hold. A score of **10** is perfect. This doesn't mean that you should give up any effort to make life happier. That is not **10**; it is just surrender. A score of **10** means you think your life is about as happy and fulfilled as any human life can be. (My hunch is that the "tens" aren't reading this book!)

Is your life satisfaction quotient lower, perhaps much lower, than you're willing to accept as your life goes on? If you have already spent considerable time and energy trying to "get it right," you may well be bringing out the verbal whips right now. But don't! Never is there a legitimate reason to cut yourself to shreds. Just the fact that you have honestly tried to look truth in the eye merits praise.

Remember, your life satisfaction quotient didn't just happen; it was *caused*. And the cause is likely to be quite complex. DLS is rooted in, and feeds back into, concrete situations that eventually form patterns. The next chapter takes a closer look at those patterns.

3

The Patterns
Behind the Plots:
A Mystery Unveiled

The patterns that underlie our experience of life are complex blends of emotions, behaviors, attitudes, and perceptions. None of these elements is as separate and distinct as we sometimes imagine, however. Life is not a collection of neat little boxes: emotions in this box, behaviors in another box, attitudes in another, and perceptions in still another. For the sake of study, we can pull them apart and examine them one by one, of course, but such an exercise doesn't reflect real life.

The following twenty "joy destroyers" comprise a mix of emotions, behaviors, attitudes, and perceptions. The mixes represent typical patterns of life for people who struggle with depressive living syndrome.

Do you see yourself in any of these personality sketches? How often does each basic belief or perception of reality cause you trouble? On a separate sheet of paper, note how often your emotions, behaviors, attitudes, and perceptions reflect that specific life pattern; indicate *Never, Seldom, Often, Usually,* or *Always.*

1) *I sense that there is more enjoyment to be had in life than I am getting.* You are not suicidal; you are not unproductive; you do not stay home alone and depressed every night. Your life is not totally empty and devoid of any joy or happiness. You have a nagging sense, however, that you are missing out on the party. There is a gremlin in the machine of your mind saying, *You missed the bus. You are standing on the B-train platform waiting for the A train.*

2) *I feel stuck.* You are basically incapable of moving on. You sense that somehow there are chains holding you in a place you do not want to be. You may recognize these chains; you may not. You have dreams, but feel powerless to pursue them. It may be the chains of the adage, "You made your own bed, now lie in it," meaning that due to some past, poor decision, you now see the "road not taken" as a heavenly city on a distant mountain. But because you feel like your feet are glued to the floor, you only dream of what never was.

3) *I find my identity outside myself.* You *are* your role, possessions, or physical looks. You are all "function": "I am *a wife*"; "I am *a husband*;" "I am *a mechanic*"; "I am *a teacher*." When your function changes (and roles always change), you are lost. Because you identify with what you have or how you look or who you are, you are in constant fear of losing your justification to even be alive. Your life is like sitting on a bubble: a guaranteed setup for worry, fear, and hostility.

4) *I tend to isolate.* You may not necessarily live in a closet, but you live without community—and so basically, you live alone. You go out and carry on a normal round of activity, but there is no one you truly share yourself with, no one who knows who you really are, no one you tell your secrets to. You may well be a magnificent giver; perhaps you're always there for others. But when you have a burning need of your own, you will ask no one to be with you. When there is an occasion for you to celebrate—a job promotion, winning a contest, having a birthday—someone else has to step forward to offer a celebration. If not, you likely will go off and celebrate alone or—more likely—just forget it. You tolerate withdrawal pangs in your own life that you will not tolerate in the lives of people you care about. You are an invisible person, forever on the fringe of supportive, shared community.

5) *I doubt my own intuition.* You have a lack of confidence. You have the tendency to hang back when your opinions and thoughts could just as well be put forth. You fear that somehow you are not as wise as others; they know something you do not. Because you do not trust your own "gut," you ignore any number of obvious (obvious to others) red flags. These flags may indicate caution with regard to relationships, business dealings, financial matters, even physical danger—but you miss them all. You miss out on the positive opportunities that hold the potential to make a marvelous difference in your life. You may see certain possibilities, but you don't have enough confidence to pursue any of them. Distrusting your intuition, you let opportunity slip by.

6) *I feel inadequate.* You put up a respectable, even a marvelous front, but inwardly you feel like a fraud. Your outside and your inside do not match. When in a group, your sense of inadequacy

screams out, "If you only knew who I really was, you would run away." Strangely, your sense of inadequacy can actually express itself in bullying, arrogant, aggressive attitudes and behaviors. Bullies are not people who think they are better than others, but those who are afraid they are not as good as others. They can and do translate this fear into all manner of abusive, cruel behavior. Either way, a deep sense of inadequacy rests at the bottom of this most difficult emotional stance.

7) *I am unlucky.* You believe that if there is anything to be won, it surely won't be won by you. You see the world as basically hostile or downright malignant; existence itself is dangerous. It is clear to you that only those born under some lucky star have a chance for any kind of blessing—and you are not one of those people. You are positively blown over at any stroke of fortune that comes your way. You are amazed to find the line in front of a movie theater shorter than you thought. You can't believe your good fortune when a snowstorm misses your city. Trapped in such a mind-set, you miss the countless blessings that in fact *do* surround you everywhere, every day.

8) *I see life as war.* You are constantly on hyperalert lest an enemy sneak up behind you. Defensiveness is your way of life. Your first judgment about any person or action is universally negative: every driver on the road is an idiot; no one on planet Earth ever acts from a motive other than profit; everyone has an angle; people will stab you in the back if you give them half a chance. There is never a justifiable reason to risk vulnerability. You think that relationships are fine as long as "they don't go too far." And "too far," for you, means any amount of commitment that would leave your heart unprotected.

9) *I never have enough time.* You live on a speeding treadmill. There is always more to be done than you can *ever* actually accomplish, which means that daily life is a chaotic rush, full of pressure. Along with the exhausting hurry you experience comes an abiding sense of guilt that somehow "more" is not being accomplished. Your calendar reflects a schedule that no one person could possibly keep up with. Being this busy, of course, means there is little or no time for yourself.

10) *I am self-critical.* Your words and thoughts about yourself are negative and critical. If you could hear every thought you had about yourself, you would hear such words as *klutz, loser, idiot,* or other self-defeating terms. You are immediately ready to take the blame for any failed effort. In fact, you absorb blame like a dry sponge.

11) *I have body shame.* You see your body as inferior enough to be an object of ridicule. You can never look good enough—and how you look is always an overriding concern. This goes beyond just wanting to look your best; this is the deep-seated belief that how you look is simply unacceptable, if not downright disgusting. You believe that you *are* your body, and your body is unacceptable—so you are unacceptable.

12) *I am the only responsible person in my life.* You are surrounded by immature, needy, or "broken" people. Although you often feel taken advantage of, you find it next to impossible to delegate or ask for help. Experience has taught you that if anything needs to be done, you're the only one who will do it. You have poor boundaries; you don't understand where your responsibilities end and another's begin. You can't understand why you feel so unloved when you're such a loving and caring person.

13) *I see gloom and doom in every circumstance.* You expect your plans—and certainly your hopes and dreams—to fall through. Hypersensitive to life's normal frustrations and disappointments, you live with a constant negative kink in your attitudes. You anticipate—and permanently cringe from—pain while at the same time you may glory in your own "endurance." You may tell endless stories about disasters of every kind. Living your life under such a black cloud, you feel very little—if any—joy. Rather, in moments of lucidity, you feel empty and alone.

14) *I am safe only if I "fit in."* Passively, out of fear that is almost self-erasing, you "go along to get along." Since conflict is so dangerous to you, you will bend over backward to maintain the appearance of a "team player," no matter how much integrity you have to compromise. As frantic as you are to "fit in" and "belong," you are, of course, often pushed around, dumped on, exploited in every way. Your transparent neediness invites such treatment. You are exhausted from laughing at jokes that aren't funny and smiling to hide your hurt. "Resentment" doesn't begin to describe the rage you feel.

15) *I never feel well enough to try anything new.* As an energy-deficient person, you have a poor diet and exercise very little. "I don't feel well" is your primary strategy for getting attention, avoiding hassles, or simply being left alone. You may go to see your doctor a great deal—if the doctor is an enabling, hand-holding type—or you may refuse to have a thorough medical examination to nail down the cause of the problem. In either event, the acceptance or cultivation of chronic "unwellness" has become your method of coping with life: *not* coping. No doubt, you do feel pretty crummy most of the time—the very lifestyle of with-

drawal guarantees it. Feeling better, let alone "good," would be too risky for you, however. It would mean you would have to get back in the game.

16) *I am too old to change.* You have lapsed into "old fogy-ism" in reaction to the bewildering changes taking place in the modern world. With each passing year, you cling tighter and tighter to "the way things used to be"—and "the way things used to be" begins to take on a deceptive, golden glow, like a still-life masterpiece in your memory. You may even pride yourself on being "out of it." You may defiantly turn your back on what is "worthless and god-awful" today in honor of a deified yesterday. It may be fairly transparent that you're rejecting a world you feel has already rejected you. You may tend to become cranky, stubborn, and rigid, or you may be sweetly benign in your refusal to make the most of the present: "Oh, no, not me. You young people go out and have a good time!" Whatever the style, though, the bottom line is the same: you've hung up your dancing shoes while the music is still playing.

17) *I have never been really close to anyone in my life.* Although you're a lonely person, you look and act like everybody else. Much like a well-trained enemy infiltrator in wartime, or the cleverly disguised space alien who passes for an earthling in a Grade B sci-fi movie, you have studied the details of "normalcy" and have mastered all the lines. You talk, laugh, have lunch with coworkers, and show up at family events. But you're faking it, every step of the way. Because you never bonded with anyone, you never really bonded with humanity itself. Deep inside, you know you are unconnected and adrift in a profound way that sets you apart. Lest anyone should know the mournful truth about you, you

sabotage possibilities of genuine intimacy as soon as another person gets too close.

18) *I am not respected.* "I get no respect!" Rodney Dangerfield's comedy routine is not so funny when disrespect is an everyday occurrence. It's devastating to be constantly discounted, pooh-poohed, ignored, or laughed at, but this is your experience of life. You find yourself in this ego-crushing predicament, and thus feel inferior to others. You don't understand why you are accorded so little status, or how you might improve your image. The pattern of ego-battering has conditioned you to play the role you seem to have been assigned. You are too demoralized to do anything else. So like a self-fulfilling prophecy, you make bad decisions, mismanage time and money, "say the wrong thing," and so forth.

19) *I couldn't endure another failure, so I don't dare try.* You have a tendency to consider yourself "finished." In your own mind, you're a dead duck, if not a collection of pulverized grease spots on the floor. Too many disappointments, too many doors slammed in your face, have made you give up on life. Regardless of your age, you've reached a point where you're just "marking time." For many people, this mind-set intensifies with the number of birthdays. Regardless of when this point is reached, the result is the same: the prospect of making a new start becomes as unlikely as walking on the moon.

20) *I don't believe in God anymore.* Your childhood images of God are responsible for much of the alienation you feel. The "big daddy" God, who never let it rain on the day of the Sunday school picnic, was nowhere to be found when some disaster struck

in your adult life. In spite of heartfelt prayers and sacrifices that hammered at the very gates of heaven, your drug-addicted son did go to prison, the tumor was malignant—or whatever. You feel abandoned, terribly let down by a God you do, indeed, believe in. But the God you are so disappointed in—even furious with—is an immature conception of a God that never did exist. Mature spirituality is not based on belief in a God who reminds us that our lost shoe is under the bottom bunk.

After you have associated *Never, Seldom, Often, Usually,* or *Always* with each pattern, assign a numerical value to each response (*Never* = 1; *Seldom* = 2; *Often* = 3; *Usually* = 4; *Always* = 5), and determine your score by adding the numbers. The higher the number, the greater the grip of DLS.

Concentrate on the last three associations—*Often, Usually,* and *Always*—noting how frequently these responses appear. For greater insight, add those three scores alone. A score higher than 50 indicates that DLS is a major factor. The higher this total, the harder the climb toward joy and liberation. Remember, however, that liberation is possible; reality is optional—at least optional in that the attitudes represented by the total of these scores can be exchanged for other attitudes.

Remember, too, that there are many joy-destroying patterns; they come in all shapes and sizes, just like human beings. Beware of judging some patterns "worse" than others without looking at the flip side. Some people who are absolutely crippled with DLS can't even imagine an ongoing sense of impending doom. Some people who constantly fight a sense of impending doom, however, would not dream of tailoring their integrity to "fit in." Yet for all our differences, we are much the same. DLS is a great leveler.

Four Identifying Characteristics

Regardless of the mixture of patterns and the expressions they take in our lives, DLS has four identifying characteristics that come together to create the cycles that create DLS. As you read, look for the presence of these telltale factors in your own life. Then try to be as specific as you can in identifying and personalizing how each characteristic exhibits itself in your everyday thoughts, feelings, and actions.

A deep sense of loss

At the core of all depression and depressive living is an abiding, if not always recognized, sense of loss. This may not be the loss of a thing, such as a house that burns down or a valuable treasure that is stolen or lost. Although such disasters certainly are losses, they are not the only or worst losses people suffer.

Notice that in each of the patterns previously sketched, there is some form of loss: a loss of self-esteem, loss of self-respect and respect for others, loss of the ability to trust, loss of dreams, loss of hope, loss of the ability to confidently plan for and pursue success. Many people experience this loss as simply the inability to see the good in life. After all, if people live under the constant burden of having to overachieve, if they cower in fear of others, if they have to fight for the most basic and fundamental of human rights, then all their energies are spent defending themselves and hiding—and it's hard to feel playful in a yard full of bullies.

If you strongly related to any of the patterns presented, ask yourself, *What loss have I incurred that makes me see myself in this pattern?* Be as specific as possible when identifying your loss.

Anger

Anger is the emotional response to a perceived injustice—and a sense of injustice is always a response to a loss: something that was mine, that should have been mine, that was mine by right, has been taken away.

Since the patterns in the sketches are learned by events repeated many times over, it is those events, smoldering in the subconscious, that feed the flame of the anger. Hidden in the dark for so long, these events often take on a texture that perhaps was not there originally. The imagined motives of others become more evil, their intention appears deliberate, and mitigating circumstances vanish. The longer the loss remains unhealed, the rougher the edges become.

Anger, like any other power, will inevitably express itself. Sometimes it boomerangs, increasing a sense of powerlessness and inadequacy. In trying to alleviate the pain, defensive behaviors are initiated that often develop into obsessional patterns, such as compulsive eating, spending, or participating in addictive relationships. The net effect of these behaviors is, of course, an ever-deepening sense of loss that, in turn, deepens the anger. Not infrequently, anger will strike outward or sideways. At these times, anyone can be the target.

Review the patterns. Notice that each pattern is guaranteed to create loss. Ask yourself, *How does my anger reveal itself?*

Paralysis

Paralysis is inevitable because nothing is done about the cycle that creates the loss that creates the anger that creates DLS. This inability to do anything may be caused by a great many things, but one of them is almost always *not recognizing* what's causing the pain.

Healing is a choice, of course, but making the choice to heal is not simply a matter of wishing away the pain. Inner conditioned patterns to choose otherwise are well learned and well practiced. The "plots" were internalized long before there existed any mature ability to pick and choose. And as these patterns were internalized, they took root in the subconscious level and quickly became habits.

It's important to recognize that habits always act to defend themselves. To ensure that these habits stay in control, people develop elaborate belief systems and self-talk scripts. As a result, these belief systems become the individual. Mental and emotional habits are no more easily dispensed with than, say, a ruptured appendix is dispensed with by saying, "I choose not to be affected by this any longer."

If people are to be empowered to change, they must first understand the life pattern and then be motivated to do what needs to be done—long enough and consistently enough to create a new habit. This is the way to acquire a new pair of glasses to view reality.

Ask yourself, *What specific habits are paralyzing me, halting my journey into the light?*

Brain chemistry

The line between the effect of brain chemistry on mood and behavior and its reverse—how mood and behavior effect brain chemistry—becomes blurred as more research is done. It seems clear now that either or both can be a true starting place. In the nonacademic world, it matters little which causes which. The point is, if there is a brain chemistry imbalance, that condition certainly needs to be addressed. But just as diabetics need to alter their diet to fit that condition, such an adjustment alone will not cure the diabetes. In fact, survival may actually depend on regular doses of insulin. In the same way, researchers are just beginning to understand the effect of certain brain chemicals on mood and behavior.

All the understanding in the world and lifestyle modifications will do little, however, if the imbalance is not addressed. Appropriate medication alone will help, but it will not heal a person's DLS. Medication simply clears the playing field so that intelligent, concrete steps can be taken toward a lasting difference. Medication will not change the "reality glasses," but it frees one's hands to change the glasses when that point is reached.

Ask yourself, *Do I suspect an element of brain chemistry imbalance in my own situation? What is there about my behavior patterns and moods that give me reason to suspect this? Should I consult my doctor? If I am taking medication, do I take it faithfully?*

Five Basic Beliefs

Recognizing our patterns and their elements is a major piece of information we can use to map out our battle against DLS. We can't fight what we can't see. Given this vital information, we need only the magic of motivation to keep us moving in the right direction. Whatever we think we can do, we usually can.

So, how do winners think? Before forging ahead, it might be encouraging to stop rooting around in our dark corners for a moment and consider the perceptions and beliefs that underlie happy, positive, peaceful lives. Are there secrets to such success?

It seems that there are certain essential beliefs that serve as cornerstones to successful living. Many great thinkers, philosophers, and saints have developed lists or formulas that reflect these basics, and have left such wisdom to us through their writings. The following five basic beliefs, reflecting the wisdom of the ages, are the building blocks of joyful living. You are encouraged to develop your own "recipe," of course.

"Life is benevolent."

For all that is wrong with you, with other people, or with the human condition in general, there is still much that is beautiful, admirable, and grand.

"I deserve a share of this benevolence."

Good things are not only "out there someplace," but out there for you. You are as deserving as anybody.

"I am capable of participating in life's benevolence."

Not only does good exist, and exist for you, but you have it within yourself to participate in that bounty.

"I can develop the skills to enjoy satisfying relationships."

You can choose not to live in isolation because you are capable of achieving loving personal relationships and full membership in a caring community.

> "It is important to leave the world
> a little better than I found it."

You intend to make a contribution, to be "part of the solution." You want the dignity of giving back more than you were given.

You can learn to be a winner at the game of life. With a better fix on the negative patterns that underlie your DLS, you are ready to move on. Next, we look "behind the scenes" at how your E-mail works.

4

Cycles Within Cycles: From Cause to Effect to Cause Again

Symptoms are not causes, not that symptoms are insignificant. Painful symptoms are real discomfort and thus merit attention. But to treat a symptom in the hope of treating the cause is to guarantee frustration and, ultimately, depression. Understanding the difference between symptom and cause can literally be a matter of life or death. The experience of one of my clients clearly demonstrates this.

From the beginning of her marriage, my client and her husband had wanted a child. Seven years into her marriage, and living on a military base, she began to experience stomach pains and was sick in the mornings. After listening to her medical history, the base doctor diagnosed her symptoms as an ulcer, and prescribed a potent medicine.

Shortly thereafter my client miscarried. The fetus was well enough developed to clearly show it was a boy. In agonizing detail, my client told me about her ride to the cemetery in a staff car and of the short, poignant funeral ceremony.

People who work hard at recovery from depressive living syndrome without understanding the difference between symptom and cause often say such things as "Why try? I'm getting nowhere." "There must be something wrong with me; I work so hard and make such little progress." "Recovery is a joke. No one ever really recovers."

Tookie and her pecan tree is a case in point. Tookie is famous for her "green thumb." She makes things grow and can save plants others can't. Her gardens and orchards are the marvel of her friends. People talk about Tookie and her "green thumb" as if some powerful god of bounty had bestowed magical powers on this graceful and powerful lady.

One day Tookie and I were standing in her beautiful yard looking at her rather shriveled pecan tree. The leaves and vines were twisted and shriveled up into what she called "witches' brooms." The nuts were deformed and ugly.

"No problem," Tookie said. "This tree just lacks zinc. I'll either spray it with zinc or feed it some zinc in fertilizer form through the ground." Then lovingly, she reached up and almost caressed the tree. "It's okay, my friend," she said. "I'll fix you up, and next year you'll have the best crop of babies you ever had."

Tookie, of course, is not magically blessed by some earth god, but she does enjoy and know a great deal about horticulture. She cared enough to go to school, learn, practice, and become very good at identifying and knowing what to do about soils, fertilizers, plants, and environmental conditions.

So what's the point? Tookie knows the difference between

causes and symptoms. She knows that the shrunken nuts on her tree are not a cause but a symptom of a problem. Understanding the difference, she doesn't go to war over the symptoms. In a sense, the symptoms are no big deal to her; the cause is. Symptoms merely indicate and point toward the real issue.

Distinguishing Between Symptom and Cause

Those of us who struggle with DLS often get tied up in knots over symptoms and leave little time or energy to seek out causes. By the very nature of the situation, our focus on symptoms means there will be little progress. Naturally, we tend to become overly frustrated, so we curse the nuts on our sick pecan tree and throw them on the ground; wrap the nuts in pretty paper to make them look better; or try to eat the nuts, pretending they're not that bad. While the poor tree tries to tell us in every way it can that it hurts, we simply get sick and tired of the darn thing giving us so much grief.

The fact is, there is something at the core of the tree that is causing the deformed fruit; the tree is begging us to understand the *meaning* of symptoms and to read the signs accurately so we can get out the zinc and ensure that next year's crop will be the best ever.

Consider these facts about symptoms:

- The importance of symptoms has to do more with what they can tell us than what they are in themselves.
- Because the pain caused by symptoms speaks in a very loud voice, it is absolutely understandable why and how symptoms tend to get all our attention and energy. And there is nothing stupid or ridiculous with

this. Taking aspirin for a headache is infinitely better than enduring hours of incapacitating pain. But if the fundamental, deep-seated condition that is the cause of the headaches is not being investigated, aspirin will only lessen the pain of the symptom for a brief period; the headaches will recur.

- Once we recognize a symptom as a symptom—and then do what we need to do to neutralize it—much of its power vanishes. Once we understand that the lack of zinc is the issue, not the shriveled nuts, there is no need to go off the deep end, expending precious energy howling about the outrage of pitiful pecans.

- Unrecognized symptoms can gang up and totally preoccupy us. Like a berserk train locomotive, one symptom can steam roll into another and another until all we can see or feel is fierce, billowing black smoke and a roaring blaze in the firebox: pain. Once this happens, there is little we can do but wait for our energy to run out. Finally, when the "train" glides to a slow—often painful—stop, we are left with our self-esteem and integrity scattered all over the track.

- When it comes to improving life, we will invariably place a great deal more energy on symptoms than we do on causes. When I mentioned this at a support-group meeting, a young woman admitted that most of her work was, indeed, targeted at symptoms. She also admitted that she wasn't sure of the difference between her symptoms and her causes.

It is crucial to accurately distinguish between symptom and cause, yet even then, when the distinction is accurately made, the cause may not be recognized through the window that the symptoms provide.

Depressive living syndrome does not have one simple cause. Rather, as with so many things in life, there are any number of complex, interconnecting factors that create the condition. In a way, our lives are like a chord of music. Many single notes come together to make the chord. To understand the blend of sounds, we must recognize and understand the single notes that make up the combination—not to mention the difference in musical instruments that produce the chord. Like musical themes, there are many systems playing in counterpoint throughout our everyday lives. Each of these systems plays out as a cluster of habits that then dictate what is normal.

Habit, of course, is whatever constitutes routine for us. And as we know, routine quickly becomes thought-*less*; we follow our routines with hardly a moment of reflection—whether it be living with or without joy, with or without DLS. The systems that support the habit guarantee it.

Just think about what's behind all the systems involved in the deceptively simple act of turning on the television. At the press of a button, we fully expect the screen to fill and the sound to come up. We don't stop to think about the detailed technology behind the picture and the sound that enter our home. We never pay the process a second thought *until it doesn't work*. Then, when there's a problem, we must either understand the system behind the problem well enough to fix it *or* hire someone who does.

We cannot hire someone to improve our lives, however. *We* are the repair person. Either we take responsibility for understanding "how it all works," or the broken part doesn't get fixed; relative to DLS, *fixed* means "healed." But healed doesn't mean "perfectly cured." The process of healing implies an empowerment to make the effective choices, based on real understanding, that enable us to take an active role in managing the powerful systems within us.

Cycles Within Cycles

The dynamics of depressive living syndrome can be demonstrated with three triangles, each one representing a cycle within itself and in relationship to the other cycles. In addition to these cycles, of course, there is always the issue of biology or brain chemistry. Biology is central to who we are, and any discussion of "cause" must include this element.

Cycle 1

Anger is at the top point of this cycle. (See next page.) Anger is about injustice, and injustice is about loss. A deep sense of loss, perhaps unrecognized, that expresses itself in anger is always involved in DLS. The anger may be building up like magma in a volcano; it may be erupting; it may be expressing itself in a far more passive way, as in a paralyzing sense of oppression. Anger wears many masks, but beneath all anger is a jagged hole where something has not only been lost, but often cruelly ripped away.

Depressive living syndrome, the manifestation of anger, is positioned at the right point of the triangle. Recall the personality profiles in Chapter 2, and all the self-defeating coping styles those profiles demonstrated. Every one of them was about anger as a result of loss: loss of hope, loss of a future, loss of our share of the pie in the sky, loss of dignity, loss of the ability to experience safety or joy, loss of the confidence it takes to create an environment for our loved ones where they will not have to learn

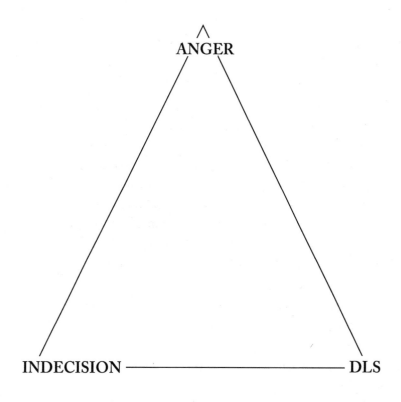

Cycle 1

such bitter lessons. Like anger, depressive living plays out in many ways.

Finally, the left point of the triangle, the resulting behavior, is indecision. For various reasons, most of us are slow to take steps–effective steps–to break an established cycle. Perhaps we simply don't know what to do, but how can we possibly know what to do if we don't know and understand what's behind the pain? Perhaps decision making is stalled because we are frustrated with having tried hard and seemingly failed. Perhaps we're not ready. Perhaps, for right now, the weight of the cycle combined with brain chemistry is so great that reading these pages is all we can manage–which, indeed, is doing something positive.

For whatever reason or mixture of reasons, the bottom line is the same. If effective, potent steps are not taken to break the cycle, the cycle remains intact. How could it be otherwise? The process is like a semitruck rolling downhill. Unless there's something to stop it, why *wouldn't* it go on rolling downhill? Physics demands it! On and on it will go until sufficient force is generated to alter its momentum.

Does Cycle 1 seem reasonable to you as you apply it to your life? Try it on. How does it square with your experience? Take each point of the triangle separately, and use it as a flashlight to shed light into your own dark corners. On a piece of paper, complete these sentences.

- My deepest sense of anger and loss comes from…
- My loss-anger suppresses itself by…
- I find it difficult to take effective action because…

Cycle 2

The pattern of Cycle 1–anger, depressive living syndrome, and indecision–is set up and supported by the three factors at work in Cycle 2. (See next page.)

There is a weight and a momentum generated by the elements in Cycle 1. (In a very real sense, these cycles are verbs, not nouns; they act and react.) One area in which the momentum of that first cycle affects us is in the social realm, positioned at the top point of the triangle.

Because it takes a lot of energy to tolerate and sustain a constant state of anger–whatever its form or face–we may be too tired to do much socializing; we would rather stay home. Perhaps we don't even know that we're isolating ourselves. To us, it seems that we are simply choosing to "sit this one out."

If the DLS expresses itself in impatience, hostility, or overt anger, we may not want to socialize because "all those idiot people out there make me crazy." We find outrageous fault, incompetence, and injury at every turn. Not being in a "state of grace," we find nothing but ugliness, insult, and intolerable frustration everywhere.

It's no news that people treat us primarily the way we treat them. That's why, if we are perpetually angry, a nasty little pattern is quickly established. The worse we treat others, the worse they treat us; the worse they treat us, the more the reason we have to treat them with ever more disrespect and disregard.

This kind of anger is hardly a victimless, private, and personal crime. In truth, we fail society when we fail ourselves in this way. Since human beings can only function fully when in relationship with others, to fail socially is to fail at a primary-life skill. Of course, the more we fail, the lonelier we become–and

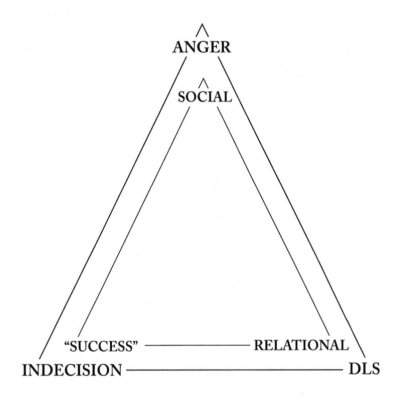

Cycle 2

the lonelier we become, the more loss we experience. The more loss, the more anger—and the cycle takes hold.

How we function socially, of course, spills over into our closer, more intimate relationships, indicated by the right point of the triangle of Cycle 2. Beyond our one-to-one romantic or sexual relationships, intimacy is about our family and close friends. These are the relationships that make up our security net.

Suppose my social failures have convinced me—and experience has borne it out—that people aren't worth loving. The fruits of intimacy, such as commitment, vulnerability, connectedness, faith, and trust, obviously are going to be impossible for me—or at least they are severely limited by my negative social orientation.

Through the ages, many wise people have said that the deepest need of the human heart is to love and be loved. In essence we *are* a hunger for love. But love in general doesn't get the job done; that's a concept like "food in general." Food in general doesn't keep us healthy; only that food which is nourishing works to keep our entire physical package fully healthy. In the same way, only love in which we personally and specifically participate has the power to spiritually and emotionally nourish us. DLS is the result of emotional and spiritual starvation.

Those of us suffering from DLS will always experience persistent and acute difficulty with intimate relationships. That difficulty—those relational problems—are both symptom and cause. Again, the lonelier we become, the more we pull away. The more we pull away, the emptier we become, and so forth.

Ultimately, DLS prevents "success," positioned at the left point of the Cycle 2 triangle. There are quotes on the word *success* because the word means different things to different people. As it is used here, the word means "accomplishment."

There is a deceptive twist on that assertion, however: one style of DLS may very well play out in perfectionistic, overachieving behavior patterns. A person with this style is powerfully driven to do more, faster, better. Enough is never enough. But the failure to accomplish is not really about just getting projects done; it's about *enjoying* the success. Overachieving may well be a compensation for a perceived loss of acceptance. In effect, the overachiever is saying, "If I make another million or buy a bigger home or have another family party, I may qualify for acceptance." If that pattern of thinking is in place, a great many projects may be accomplished, but little will be enjoyed.

For many, however, our problem is not about overachieving. Rather, we struggle with a huge sense of inadequacy as a result of too many failed social and relational efforts. For us, isolation has become our main coping technique. Not that we necessarily stay in our homes twenty-four hours a day, and not that we don't have friends. But we never really "go out" of ourselves. We never really get close to anyone. We keep secrets, the biggest of which is ourselves. Whether we blame this pattern on our own inadequacy or turn it around and blame it on the inadequacies of others, the net result is the same. Alone is alone.

Whether in fear or constant rage, we don't try. After a while we even get too tired to think about trying. If anyone suggests that we set goals, we immediately reject the idea as "stupid" or "okay for others." The posting for a promotion at work is passed over—"Maybe next time." The opportunity to enroll in an interesting new class, participate in a study club, or begin a small savings account is automatically put off. Sometimes we do this calmly, and sometimes we experience rolling emotions. Sometimes we tell ourselves, *It's all a set up anyway. It just isn't fair. I'd never be able to do that.* But if we try to figure out *what* is a set up, *what* isn't fair, or *why* we're unable to do something, our thinking gets confused and generalized: EVERYTHING *is a set up.* EVERYTHING *is unfair. I can't do* ANYTHING. This is the cycle.

Personalize Cycle 2 to your own life. On a piece of paper, write your responses to these questions.

- What social limitations do I experience as a result of depressive living syndrome? Considering my life satisfaction quotient, and focusing on the system that created that score, how do these systems affect me socially?
- How is my relational competence limited by depressive living syndrome? As I shine the light of intention on the quality of my personal relationships, what do I find? To what extent are my relationships satisfying or not satisfying? What system do I see working beneath the surface?
- How is my ability to accomplish and enjoy success limited by depressive living syndrome? Is the problem a genuine lack of achievement or the limited ability to enjoy it? How is this element played out in my life?

Remember, these are systems within systems, cycles within cycles. Our tendency as Westerners, which is to say analyzers, is to separate everything into its parts, describe each part, and call the bucket of parts "reality." Many of us have a very difficult time seeing things in relationship, realizing that one thing causes another and in turn is caused by it. We can examine a moment or an event in our lives in minute detail, and yet fail to recognize that in the moment, all that detail is experienced instantaneously.

In that same complex fashion, all these systems affect one another. Social, relational, and success issues are directly affected by anger, DLS, and indecision. Each is grist for the mill of another. The more failure experienced in Cycle 2, the greater the sense of loss that translates into depressive, joy-limited life.

From these systems then comes the third cycle.

Cycle 3

Depressive living syndrome is always grounded in and justified by negative mental processes, situated at the top point of Cycle 3. (See next page.) After all, we are the way we think: a truth that has been a psychological basic for centuries. The important perspective, however, is to see the content of our thinking in the context of these cycles. Gripped by loss and anger, we can easily come to feel that others are out to get us. Given this, isolation and withdrawal from satisfying social connections are hardly surprising responses.

It doesn't take a genius to guess the content of our mental processes when our behavior indicates withdrawal. If we could only hear our own inner dialogue, we could easily see how it fashions our outer world. An orange placed before a mirror will never reflect an apple; it will always reflect an orange. In the same way, show me your outer world, and I will tell you the nature of your inner world; one cannot be different from the other.

Keeping a journal of inner dialogue has been a staple activity at personal-growth workshops for many years. Participants are told to periodically record the thoughts flashing through their minds. Clearly it's a good idea to listen in on the electric chatter that clutters up the neural pathways in our minds. This chatter

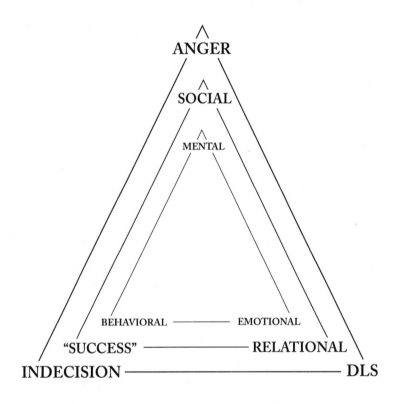

Cycle 3

dictates the quality of our daily lives, even though most of us are totally unaware of its content.

Self-talk is a very accurate barometer. Passive people think passive thoughts; angry people think angry thoughts; fearful people think fearful thoughts; perfectionistic people think thoughts that reinforce their sense of inadequacy, and so forth.

Situated at the right point of the triangle is our emotional world. Just as a steady stream of water powers a waterwheel, so all our negative thinking creates a steady stream of negative emotion. In another sense, of course, there *are* no negative emotions. *All* of our feelings are part of who we are—even painful, difficult feelings need to be recognized and accepted. Labeling any emotion as "bad" can impel us to shy away (or run away) from the truth about ourselves. And as we run, the mouse becomes the lion. How much wiser to be open to *all* our emotions so we can integrate them into the whole of our personality. Why? Because, once integrated, no renegade emotion can so dominate our existence that we're forced to center our lives around it.

The emotional rhythms of our life are *caused*, flowing naturally from what goes before and what comes after. Our behavioral responses, then, positioned at the left point of the triangle, respond to reality as we see it. Even the most insane among us are but responding to reality as we see it. If we see pink elephants running around, it makes all the sense in the world—to us—to get out of the way. The real problem is not about dodging elephants, however, but about what makes us see the elephants in the first place.

What is our reality? How do we see the world in which we live? Look to the cycles. We see the world through the eyes of our cycles. Does the cycle at work in us demand that we constantly do more to somehow win the prize of self-justification?

Then, of course, our behavior will reflect that dictate. We will always be busy, glorying in how much we can accomplish. While others play, we will be forever responsible–staying loyal to our cycle. There will always be a reason why we can't just sit down and take it easy along with everybody else.

Secretly–until we get ready to make some change–we will think less of those who don't work as hard as we do. Our inner dialogue will reflect and create that attitude. But when fatigue catches up, we will envy those who seem to have so much more fun than we do. We will wonder how it is that they seem so carefree in life while we are always buried under responsibility.

Our cycles are our eyeglasses. If our cycles translate into a fearful stance toward life, our behavior will follow along as surely as the tail follows the dog down the street. Wherever we go, fear will pull our wagon along as well as any handle could: fear, as both cause and consequence.

The action necessary to confront unacceptable behavior in others will be torturous or impossible for us. "Going along" will feel a whole lot better. As a result, we will slip into a kind of emotional prostitution that will do anything to avoid conflict. We simply can't take the risk that others might become angry with us. As we act out our fear, we think more fearful thoughts, thus entrenching our fearful stance toward life. Inevitably, that much fear affects our accomplishments, which affect our sense of loss and anger.

Personalize this third and last cycle. On a piece of paper, write your responses to these questions.

- What are my habitual patterns of thinking? In what direction do my thought-habits lead me?

- What is the connection between my thoughts and my feelings? Specifically, how do my negative thoughts reinforce my negative emotions? What emotions do I most commonly experience in my daily walk through life? What thoughts are these emotions associated with?
- When I look in the areas that I find most depressing or anxiety-ridden, what are my behavior patterns? When I look behind the behavior and emotional elements, can I see what mental pattern is at work? What are my social, relational, and "success" issues? Do I have an abiding sense of loss, a typical DLS lifestyle, and an inability to make positive decisions?

The Total and Complex "I"

At the core of this is "I," the "I" that is you, the incredibly complex, born-for-love-and-community person that you are, walking through your short stay on planet Earth. "I" has a face and hands, a body shape, and vocal tones—and they all look like and sound like yours. "I" is as old as you are, and works to maintain an image that you want to portray. And behind all of this unique personhood are the cycles that support and cause who "I" is—in and of yourself as well as in relation to others and the world around you. (See next page.)

The dynamics of these cycles are as mysterious to us as the mystifying switch-turning and pump-starting and voltage-regulating of a car. We never think about how it all works; we just get in, fire it up, and drive away. In a way, we, as human beings, are not so different. Every day we fire up and drive away into our lives. But just as a well-running car is the collection of many well-running parts, so is the quality of our existence. If

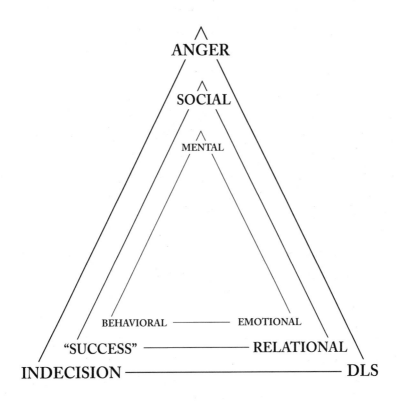

The Total and Complex "I"

our lives are tainted by depressive living syndrome, we can fix that—if we are motivated to take responsibility for those cycles that cause the malfunction. And let there be no misunderstanding about that—DLS *is* a malfunction. It is not the way we—any of us—were made to live our lives.

5

The Problem Behind
the Problem:
The Big Empty

S ome of the unexpected detours of life come at us in the form of chronic anxiety, depression, chemical dependency, toxic habituations, hyper-vulnerability to stress-induced illnesses, obsessive/compulsive disorder, and a host of other "labeled" dysfunctions.

How many suffer from such problems? The National Institute of Mental Health reports that in any given year nearly a fourth of the population of the United States is diagnosed with some form of these ailments. The tranquilizer Xanax is so commonly prescribed for people suffering chronic anxiety that it has become the fifth most prescribed drug in the country–far ahead of antibiotics or birth control.

It would be surprising if all the "labeled" people *did not* struggle with depressive living syndrome in some way. Of course, many more "unlabeled" people are also trapped in some self-perpetuating, joy-destroying (or at least limiting) pattern.

A central element of all these misery-producing patterns, whether they carry a formidable label or not, is the battered, wounded, starving ego: our core. Obviously, it is not within the scope of this book to offer an in-depth treatment of any of the particular categories listed above, but rather to "spread the net" in our discussion of DLS to include those who have diagnosed ailments as well as those who do not. Whether or not these labels apply doesn't really matter. The key issue is the effect that all these conditions have on the quality of our lives. Although labeling is the arbitrary identification of statistical information, there is one common denominator: all these labels indicate situations that emotionally and spiritually gut people. No matter what we call them, these disorders ruin lives.

If we can understand the connection between these various situations and the underlying models of DLS, we move toward conquering those demons that keep us from celebrating life. What else could Jesus have meant when he said, "I came that [you] may have life, and have it abundantly" (John 10:10)?

Academics make some fine and accurate distinctions between these labels and categories. They say that addiction, by definition, includes tissues addiction. Such would be the case with dependence on alcohol or crack. In such clear, physical addictions, our very tissues scream out to be satisfied, the cellular receptor sites having become irritated lions.

Habituation, academics say, has many of the characteristics of addiction, but does not include tissues addiction. This would be the case with compulsive gambling or sexual addiction. In other words, there is no direct-related substance involved. Yet some force within these "habituated" people becomes powerful enough to take control of their lives, relentlessly pushing them into an ever darker, more desperate place.

Whether one's situation is addiction or habituation, the power is there to ruin a life. However valid the distinction may turn out to be, we just don't know enough to assume that, with habituation, there is not some form of brain chemistry imbalance that is very, very close to, say, opiate addiction. Either way the hair may be split, those who have fallen into these pits are in lethal trouble. The resulting misery is the same.

Does the shoe fit? Think about the four most common areas of obsessive/compulsive behavior: food, money, relationships, and busyness. Like the old "cement boot" of hoodlum lore, all of these expressions of the same pattern will effectively anchor the victim to the bottom of the river. It's more a matter of choosing your poison than anything else.

Identifying Common Traits

As an overarching frame of reference for these seemingly unlike situations, consider five common traits or characteristics that are often used to indicate the presence of addiction, habituation, or obsessive/compulsive behaviors. Again, there certainly are differences among these expressions—they are not exactly the same—but the common traits indicate a common bottom line.

Preoccupation

Whatever the particular expression of distress, we are never far from thinking about it. Those of us who have problems with compulsive gambling, for example, are always thinking about the next bet or where to place it. Those of us whose relational problems center around the unending pursuit of the next conquest constantly think about the next who, how, when. Scarcely anyone of the opposite sex is safe with us because each individual is a challenge to pursue and conquer rather than a human being. Not that this is a freely made choice; it isn't. We desperately may wish with all our heart that the enormous pressure inside us would let go. But it's always there, like a yellow-eyed wolf prowling the back ways of our mind. For us, that wolf is never fully out of sight.

Along with preoccupation comes all the associated scheming, dodging, lying, rationalizing—whatever it takes to keep the "supply" coming. Nothing causes panic like the possibility that the "pain reliever of choice" might become unavailable. Our palliatives become a way of existence—a substitute for life.

These kinds of fixations are the source of stories and, all too often, dark jokes, like the one about the alcoholic who prepares to enter the treatment center by seeding the entry grounds with bottles; or the newcomers to weight-reduction facilities who devise ingenious ways to keep a ready supply of sweets available. Obviously, some humor can be drawn from these situations. But the need, the hurt, and the emptiness that fuel these expressions of uncontrolled pain are not at all funny. There is no amusement in the tragic loss of self-esteem that always follows such addictions.

Loss of control

Those of us who can relate to being stuck in one of these pits know the trauma of loss of control. Time after time, we make the "never-again" commitment—and time after time, the behavior happens again. Repeatedly, heroically even, the demon may be faced and the resolve painted in ten-foot high letters: I'LL NEVER PUT MYSELF IN THIS SITUATION AGAIN. But it doesn't take long for the letters to fade, and we "slip."

Does it matter if we call such strangleholds "addictions," "habituation," or "obsessive/compulsive disorder"? No; strangled is strangled. Whether the object of all that toxic energy is substance related or behavior—the endless counting of telephone poles, checking and rechecking the doors at night to make sure they are locked, constant handwashing—the ability to simply say "no" vanishes and life becomes a nightmare. With the effective paralysis of free will, words cannot describe the experience of guilt and loss. Eventually, that loss triggers the anger that signals the toxic mental parade that generates increasingly hurtful emotions that kicks off a repetition of destructive behavior that....And always at the center of the cycle lies the victimized sense of self.

This loss of control is the element in the pattern that people who are not so trapped find nearly impossible to comprehend. It is this befuddlement that produces the often-heard remark, "If he(she) really loved me, he(she) would stop." But the "pull" is beyond love—and even beyond one's innate survival instinct. That is the real "loss," the ultimate price paid for falling into this pit. Once freedom of choice is gone, self-esteem soon follows. The vacuum left, like a black hole in outer space, sucks all joy into itself.

Have you ever vowed, "never again," feeling certain that you would succeed—only to find the wolf looking at you, mockingly, at the next turn in the road?

Tolerance

Tolerance refers to the progressive nature of the pull. With time, it takes more and more of the behavior to achieve less and less relief. One drink is enough for a while, but then it takes two or three to feel brave (or less afraid). Comforting your loneliness with a slice of pie turns into hiding the whole pie in your bedroom. And with each step along the downward slope, the cycle deepens. The process is like feeding a fire–the flames grow ever hotter.

We cannot overestimate the power of the pull. For example, simply eliminating the situation that triggers the pattern of slavery does not arrest the cause of the DLS. Think about someone who acts out his or her hurt through addictive relationships. That person cannot simply refrain from all contact with the opposite sex, and then claim to be healed after a year or two. As sure as a lit match on dry leaves always creates fire, the first time that individual gets involved again, the same old yellow-eyed enemy will appear; nothing will have changed. Removing the temptation doesn't touch the cause of the problem. More often than not, in fact, the deferred attraction will be as strong as if the abstinence never took place; even in the absence of acting out the behavior, the compulsion's place in the psyche is secure.

Withdrawal

True tissue addiction is not a bit subtle. When the substance that the cells have learned to depend on is taken away, there is a revolt; the body responds to its denial. Serious coffee drinkers who are somehow denied their fix know only too well how their bodies go into withdrawal. The same is true of sugar-satiated people. Deprive the cells that are accustomed to swimming in sugar, caffeine, or nicotine, and the hound of hell starts yelping in their innards. It is a common experience. Even when tissue addiction is not a factor, there is the pull of psychological addiction. Old habits form strong chains—chains that will resist even the sharpest teeth of a saw.

Delusion and denial

Common to all seductive patterns is the element of delusion and denial. Until the discomfort caused by these patterns is great enough, we simply are not willing to give them up. So what do we do? To dodge the unmistakably clear mandate for drastic action, we cloud reality.

One effective way to do this is to refuse to give accurate names to what is going on. Sometimes we even give virtuous or cute names to our trap. We call ourselves a "chowhound," not a food addict; a "ladies' man," not a sex addict. We claim to be "responsible" or "willing to go the extra mile" when the truth is, we are so desperate for approval that we're unable to say no, even if someone wants to set our hair on fire! We are "daring" or "like to live on the edge" when in fact, full-blown money issues are eating us alive.

Such delusion and denial, of course, creates paralysis in our main, innermost cycle. And it is this paralysis that prevents the decision making that could break the cycle. Our ability to delude and deny eventually creates a wall between us and reality, allowing no chance for us to take a stand against the causal patterns.

So what happens? Depressive living syndrome falls around us and in us like the darkest Arctic night that knows no dawn.

Do any of these five traits ring a bell? Think before you answer. Your truthful answer to this question is not about self-indictment. The point is consciousness raising, not guilt deepening. There is empowerment in understanding. To *see* is the prerequisite of taking a stand.

How foolish we are to curse ourselves when self-attack only deepens the pattern that holds us down. The real problem is not with some power or substance *outside* ourselves; rather, something *inside* is "the problem behind the problem." Of course, we are *more* than these patterns, but the delusion and denial of calling these patterns something other than what they are is literally nonsense. Such game-playing destroys us.

We Were Made for Love

So what is the true source of this toxic power? Exactly where is the pit? If at the center of our cycle stands our core—"I" at my deepest level—then that surely is where the power is born, be it destructive or creative. For as long as our species has had the ability to exercise intelligence and thought, great thinkers, philosophers, poets, saints, and scholars have been saying that we were made for love, that our very nature is social, that we need one another. In fact, academics have built levels, scales, and an entire language around this basic truth, and empirical data gathered from countless clinical experiments have proven the point.

Do you remember the famous experiment that studied the infant mortality rate? Infants were given every need-fulfillment except the nurturing touch of a mother. The babies fared poorly. When this need for intimacy was fulfilled, however, this crucial "medicine"—the tactile nurturing, the sound of a beating heart, the warmth of closeness—worked like magic; the babies' health improved dramatically.

When those deepest of human needs—the need to love, be loved, and belong—are denied, the pit is dug, and the deficit of intimacy creates chaos. This is true regardless of what the contributing factors of biology and brain chemistry may be, either as cause or result, or in the continuous recycling of both. Like a powerful bow being drawn back, the more that intimacy is deprived, the more power is transferred to the potential for chaos.

Humans, of course, are infinitely varied. Some, it seems, can take the most depressing beginning and translate that energy creatively. Somehow they are able to channel the deepest pool of anger in a positive direction. Much of the world's great art is the energy of pain made beautiful. Although this magnificent art is expressed in a physical medium, such as paint or stone, more often it shines in the quality of a life and the content of a character. Most of us, however, are not that exceptional. We come up with a mixed bag.

The Big Empty

The "Big Empty": I have heard this phrase used to describe the hole left by intimacy deprivation. I have also heard intimacy deprivation described as a throbbing, bleeding, jagged wound. Whatever the image, the resulting pain of intimacy deprivation will always seek to heal itself. Sometimes, as in our compulsions, the energy goes in the wrong direction.

A telling saying in Alcoholics Anonymous is that everyone who empties a bottle is looking for God at the bottom. A gentleman at a self-help meeting used a different, but equally helpful, analogy. Think of King Kong, he suggested, grabbing a tube of toothpaste and giving it a squeeze. You can bet the toothpaste is going to come cascading out. Some will come out of the top, some out of the bottom, some out of the sides. The point is not about where the tube breaks when King Kong squeezes it, but why it breaks.

That image makes a world of sense when you think about it. Is it more important to patch the tear, or to get Mr. Kong's hand off the tube?

If the basic need for love and acceptance lies at the center of our core, that which denies this need sends out toxic ripples through our whole system of cycles. It's bad enough to find ourselves trapped in one of these cycles, but it's even worse to heap on guilt, shame, and blame. If we don't feel well, we don't act well. Release from DLS–not just a momentary ripple of relief–demands that we take dead aim at the Big Empty within. No matter what the specific issue, you may be sure that it is there, lurking beneath all expressions of obsessive/compulsive behavior.

An example from each of the four most common areas of obsessive/compulsive behavior–food, money, relationships, and busyness–will demonstrate the savage pain of the Big Empty, and the tremendous work needed to take dead aim at it.

Food

Obviously, food fixations come in different forms: bulimia, anorexia, a combination of both, and the addiction to overeating are among the most common. All may be affected by brain chemistry. But surely, at the core of the core, is the yawning chasm of the Big Empty. A crushed ego is the major element in every addictive behavior.

I introduce you to Karen. When I knew her, she was twenty-one years old, absolutely beautiful, first in her class at college, with everything imaginable to look forward to—and bulimic unto death. Karen came from a family of three sisters and one brother. Her father died shortly after he arrested his alcoholism. He had been a wealthy lawyer.

Through many years of E-mail, Karen internalized an unshakable belief that she was not worthy. When she looked at herself, she saw only a pitiful, inadequate human being who had gotten just what she deserved. It's an old story. The more she tried, the more she accomplished—and the more she accomplished, the more she felt she needed to accomplish. The pressure built.

No one knows what tipped Karen's scales toward food, but that is the coping technique she used. Food helped her find relief from her inner demons. Yet, even as she gorged herself, her toxic E-mail came in torrents, barraging her with guilt, shame, fear, self-hatred, and terrible explosions of anger. Negative emotion poured over her like magma down the side of a volcano. Her bulimia, she said, was her punishment. Being such a terrible person, she deserved this kind of humiliation—which was even more poignant for being self-imposed.

Through the whole ordeal, Karen remained frantically busy. She was terrified of slowing down. Why? Because she might encounter herself. Her core was torn to shreds. The more she tried to stop the pattern of binge-purge, the more wounded she became. King Kong was in full control of the tube.

Lots of people from alcoholic families do not develop food addictions, but Karen did. For whatever combination of reasons, the magical, mystical mechanism at her core turned to the comforting embrace of food.

Looking at Karen, you never would have suspected a food problem. She was slender, but not gaunt. She could laugh and dance with the best of them. Her secret self ventured out only in the stillness of night. Quiet was her mortal enemy.

Try to consider the loss in Karen's life, as seen through her inner eye. What did it matter to her that most people saw her as lucky, even blessed? Only she knew that she had experienced great loss in her life: loss of a father figure, loss of a reliable source of warmth that had been important to her, loss of the security of knowing that both parents were available to love her. Loss at every turn. Think of the fearful, threatening, grieving messages, loud and early, that zoomed through her cycles. These sharp-edged negative messages cut slivers from her core as they spiraled downward. Remember, every hurt will seek to heal itself.

Karen's story had a happy ending. As she came to understand the nature of her obsession, she was empowered to make different choices. It wasn't easy; it never is. The more she practiced those behaviors that built up her core, the less need she had for the false healing of addictive behavior. Slowly, she climbed out of the pit. She learned not only to honor rather than damage herself, but to understand the difference between love and addiction.

Money

As with food, compulsive money issues take many shapes of misuse and abuse. Some people act out their obsessive/compulsive behavior through gambling, others with wild spending, and still others with hoarding. Some people don't believe they are worthy or capable of making enough money to live on. Now watch the twist of logic here: while these people are constantly suffering from insufficient funds, they continue to sabotage any efforts to create genuine financial well being.

Although his situation is but one of a thousand, Donald gives us an instructive example. Donald is forty-nine years old, divorced for the second time. He's quiet, sweet-natured, an entirely likable man—unless you happen to be married to him. Donald is a compulsive spender. Brain chemistry? Perhaps—even probably. But true to form, Donald learned harsh self-definition early on from an extremely demanding father. According to his father, Donald was a "screw-up." There was absolutely nothing Donald could do right. As a result, there was nothing Donald would not do to glean the tiniest grain of acceptance from his father. Perhaps the terms *glean* and *grain* come to mind because Donald and his father were farmers. The confidence-crippling E-mail sailing around Donald's cycles suggested that if he *had* enough, he would *be* enough.

Unlike many other compulsive spenders, however, Donald never went in for glitzy, high-priced merchandise. He never bought a Rolex watch or a Cadillac. Rather, Donald went into the kind of irrational debt that would gain his father's acceptance; he bought stock, acreage, and machinery.

Even when the price of beef plummeted, Donald bought more and more stock—on credit, of course. Then he bought more acreage, then more outbuildings and more machinery. The deeper in debt he sunk, the more pressure he felt. King Kong at the controls again! To catch a few moments of relief, Donald reached out in the only way he knew how. He wanted to make his father proud of him. Karen binged and purged; Donald bought more stuff.

I worked with Donald and his second wife, Helen, who came to the marriage with considerable proceeds from the sale of her house. Trying to be a good team player, Helen made that money available for Donald's purchases, even though she questioned his good judgment. "I thought he knew something I didn't," she explained. Later Helen realized that it wasn't what Donald didn't *know* that did them in, but what he didn't *feel*—and what he did feel was the aching pit of the Big Empty.

Donald finally admitted that his endless purchases did not make rational sense. With a great deal of inner work, he came to realize that almost every aspect of his life had been created around the desperate hole in his core.

While his overbearing father lived, Donald always sided with his father in every issue, regardless of the conflict. Even in middle age, Donald simply never achieved separation from his father. Again, lots of people have grown up with overbearing parents and have not gone this route, but Donald did. And it's not a bit useful to say that Donald was "weak" or "should have known better." Rather, understand that such expressions of compulsive/obsessive behavior are hard-wired into the negative cycle. The bow, for Donald, was bent back to the breaking point. When his arrow was released, it flew directly into the toxic bull's eye.

Interestingly enough, Donald, Helen, and I had a session with Donald's brother. As the oldest of the family, this brother had received the largest and choicest portion of the farm when the father's estate was divided. The brother could not understand why Donald was in therapy. It was utterly beyond him. "Donald must be stupid. I grew up in the same environment he did, and I haven't been hurt by any of this 'intimacy deficit nonsense.' In fact, I have no real problems at all."

Well, I will tell you this: a more hostile, hurt, angry man would be hard to find. The brother had no idea why his two sons were drug dependent and his daughter had run away from home as a teenager. It would never occur to him that his children's behaviors had anything whatsoever to do with him.

I don't know how Donald's story is unfolding today. Although he was making progress, he stopped coming to see me when his marriage broke up and he lost his section of the farm. My hope is that he has somehow learned to listen to his inner music and discovered beauty there.

Relationships

Many people are addicted to the experience of love: relationships. How many ways are there to be addicted to love? Count them. For some, it takes on the behavior of sexual addiction. These people are compelled by the chase and the capture. They care little or nothing for the relationship itself. For others, it is an addiction to pornography. Many find a hook in their one-to-one relationships; they cannot tolerate being alone. Their identity is totally tied up with being part of a "couple." Until they are involved in a relationship, even a toxic one, they are in torment. Any self-worth they experience is contingent upon the fact that they are in a relationship. Think about it. Doesn't it seem that every TV comedy series has at least one such sex or love addict as a central figure? On the surface, a lot of the love addicts' predicaments can seem very funny. But the surface is not very thick.

Tony, like Karen and Donald, is a nice person. On the outside he is sharp and in control. Tony has a lot going for him. He is in his mid forties—tall, thin, handsome, and quite well off.

The inside is a different story, however. Tony doesn't know if his father was an alcoholic. He does know that he was very young when his father abandoned the family. His mother was apparently a religious neurotic. To her, everything was a sin. "God is watching you," was her constant warning. Tony learned early that he could never be quite good enough, though God knows he tried. (God does know.)

Perhaps it was Tony's innate sense of vulnerability that set him up. Maybe it was his good looks. Whatever the contributing details, girls and women were strongly drawn to him. His first sexual experience was in eighth grade. It was then that Tony realized two amazing things. For a short amount of time, sex provided an escape from the crushing guilt and pressure that constantly dogged him—and sex felt good. His "sinful" act had a further payoff: it proved that he was a miserable wretch!

Tony can't remember all the women he's had sexual relationships with. Never did he use force; never did he physically coerce anyone; never did he intend to hurt anyone. But his pattern of addictive "chase" left his life in tatters—as well as the lives of many of the women he conned over the years. Conquest by conquest, Tony learned to lie and cheat, to cover up and tell only half-truths. Of course, his integrity diminished as his little black book grew fat. If the feminist movement wanted someone to hang a bull's eye on, Tony was the guy.

Tony is working on his E-mail. He is racked by guilt over the damage he has done to himself and others—especially his three wives and four children. But blame and guilt are not the point. Conquering DLS depends on understanding. I have walked through some very dark places with Tony, to the depths of his crushed core. Incident after incident, not substantially different from Karen or Donald, Tony told of intense feelings of inadequacy and shame. He talked about his desperation as a kid when there was no one to talk to and no one at home he could trust. He remembered feeling terrible when he stole a car and took it for a joy ride as a teenager. "Somehow, I just had to let out that rage that was inside." Tony admits to fits of weeping, after conning some lonely woman into a relationship or a one-night stand. Crying in the dark after sex–all in the name of "love."

Tony actually insisted that I take his little black book as a symbol of his commitment to turn his life around. In that book were not only the names of the women he had contact with in various towns, but the names he used for himself in those towns. His addiction had so complicated his life that he had to keep track of "who he was" in any given place. He had so many names, he couldn't remember all of them.

When Tony and I met for the first time, he said he wanted to build himself up spiritually. But there can be no spiritual growth until the demons residing in the Big Empty are addressed. Until that is done, the negative behavior will continue generating incredible amounts of shame, blame, and guilt. Light cannot shine through layer after layer of guilt and shame.

Busyness

Busyness may seem the weakest of the four examples of addictive behaviors. Food, money, and relationships or "love" addictions seem awfully big time in comparison; they are capable of truly destroying life. But busyness? Who doesn't have too much to do? Who isn't overbusy? Do we have a choice? Well–do we?

Many people could profit by asking themselves this question. Some people endlessly have too much to do–endlessly. They seem incapable of saying "no," so they chronically overextend themselves. When occasions arise that would allow for rest, they find a way to subvert the possibility. Ultimately, these people internalize their E-mail in such a way that they are only "good" to the degree that they can "accomplish." The hidden hook, of course, is that there is no such thing as "enough." So enough can never be accomplished. Consequently, there is absolutely no way these people can ever justify feeling good about themselves. If this brutal busyness—and the exhaustion that inevitably follows—does not deepen DLS, nothing will.

Addicted to busyness comes in many varieties. The all-time classic, of course, is the wife-mother-homemaker whose collective tasks are indeed staggering. This devoted and dutiful woman lets her own life go as she juggles everyone else's. In the absence of a separate and distinct existence—except in her roles as servant and facilitator—she gradually comes to define herself as she is defined, ticking items off her to-do list with a saintly vengeance. But task-ticking hardly makes a complete life. Deep down inside, her ego is not fooled; in fact, it's in a state of constant, if subtle, revolt.

Professionals in the human services—counselors, nurses, social workers, and the like—are vulnerable to joy-squelching busyness. Their intentions are the best, and their causes are as noble as they are real. Yet, so often, the very drama and desperation of their clients' circumstances compel these professional helpers to give away everything they have—and then some. Personal lives get pushed back into the deepest corner of a back shelf, and ordinary self-care becomes a wistfully dreamed of luxury on the order of a Mediterranean cruise. They're just "too busy for it."

The unmet needs of these people often change form in a desperate attempt to be noticed. Migraine headaches, frequent and vague illnesses, and early job burnout are just a few of the common manifestations.

Cal, for example, is a wheeler-dealer, a self-made man who has a hand in more business projects than any three energetic people would be willing to undertake. So what if Cal is smart and creative; so what if everyone who knows him tells admiring stories of his business acumen; so what if he "proved himself" years ago? None of that alters the fact that he is socially isolated, emotionally needy, and spiritually starving. Nothing in Cal's amazing track record has been enough to compensate for what he's missed.

Not surprising, Cal's relationships with women have been disappointing. Even those who most hankered after the material benefits of marriage to such a man eventually got tired of the cellular-phone conversations during dinner, the business trips that preempted special occasions, and his sheer inability to ever leave work at work. Cal realizes now that he missed the boat, although he is only just beginning to figure out why.

Right now Cal is on square one, beginning at the beginning. I hope he will continue his journey long enough to slow down. If hurry, vim, and vigor were the horses that would carry him to happier territory, he would have long since been there. But peace of mind is not a prize that can be run down and overcome with fast talk.

Karen fixed on food, Donald on money, Tony on uncommitted love, and Cal on unrelenting busyness. All of them took off early, running like mad toward something—anything—to divert and distract them from facing the horror of the Big Empty. They are not "dumb" or "crazy" or "evil" people, as they sometimes call themselves in fits of self-loathing and despair. Every one of them would have used better, healthier coping techniques if they'd only known how.

Today, all four have a chance for happiness that they didn't have before. If they keep going forward, they will get there—just as we will if we do the spadework that is necessary for the saving grace of healing to bloom in our hearts.

6

Healing and Recovery: Time to Move On

Our inner houses may well have a few ghosts and shadows, but these "residents" need not be in control. They may serve as thermometers that measure our internal status quo, but they do not have to be thermostats that control our inner environment. How much sunshine we allow into our houses is ultimately up to us. That is what healing is all about.

In popular usage *healing* means "no longer wounded." When we speak of being healed of a disease, we mean that the disease is no longer present in our body. Our life can progress as if nothing happened: we can get back on the slopes and race away.

But there is another, deeper meaning of the word *healing*. That meaning has less to do with injuries disappearing and more with the acceptance of that which will never disappear. It has to do with the sufficient deepening of our spirit to a point where the injury is incorporated into the whole spectrum of our personality. When this happens, the injury still exists, but it no longer dictates the quality of our life. This kind of healing means growth to the point of saying, "Yes, it did happen, this is so. I accept it, but it is not the only thing that is so!" Such acceptance creates a sense of peace amidst the chaos, and allows the experience of serenity to be as real as the experience of rage.

Healing in the Big Empty

The damage behind depressive living syndrome is not caused by virus or bacteria. It is not the result of an automobile accident or a birth defect. The long-running toxic E-mail that creates a negative perception of reality is caused by injury to our deepest selves. The healing that needs to take place is located in the center of the Big Empty. That wounding was not caused by random, impersonal fate, but by our human and natural vulnerability to people we loved who gave us scorpions instead of bread. Intentionally or not, the ghosts and shadows that bedevil us, the ones that hide the sun, came into being long ago when we most needed to be accepted and affirmed. Because of them, at least in our own perception, we were left outside the ring of light and warmth.

With our flesh and bones, we stand behind our high score on DLS traits or patterns. Within us the cycles function, constantly reinforcing one another and reinforcing the traits. It could be said that at the core of the cycles is the canvas upon which we—our real selves—are sketched. Whatever in us translates into DLS is stained by the pigments and tones of wasted love. In professional jargon, this is often called *intimacy deficit*. Within our personal thought patterns, it's called self-talk: *All I ever wanted was to be loved. Why wouldn't you love me?*

Understanding this process is not about blame; it's not about abandoning our own responsibility by accusing another for our deficiencies. In all probability, those who failed us loved us to the full extent of their capabilities. Rather, this process is about claiming responsibility for the quality of our lives *today*, something that can only be accomplished by understanding the dynamic process that currently diminishes our ability to enjoy life. Central to that understanding is the undeniable fact that we are all made for love and acceptance. When that is denied, we are in trouble. Where acceptance is deficient, the ground is stony, and thus the harvest will be one of weeds rather than blossoms.

After all is said and done, it ill suits any of us to make judgments about another. Why a particular deficit is exhibited in a particular manner in one person's life and takes a different form in another is not useful or important information. What is important is to keep our eyes focused on our own lives. What is easy or no problem for us may be a major difficulty for another. The trick is to keep going, don't stop, because the other side of the coin is equally true: what is difficult for us may be a piece of cake for someone else. The point is not *where* the toothpaste tube ruptures, but *why*. Progress comes when we forget about anyone else and look at our *own* ghosts and shadows.

We begin by giving names to our ghosts and shadows, and identifying their birthplace. Suppose we were to write down our story, including where our hurt came from. What was the "gut shot" for us, individually? Where was our severest wound inflicted, and by whom?

The intensity of the replay may well be overwhelming. Some of us will focus on how we felt a lack of value within a family system: "I know you (parents) always loved me, but I never thought you loved me as much as you loved Jimmy. He was your favorite. I was always second best." Some of us will report gender rejection: "My original sin was being born female. No matter what I did or how well I did it, it just didn't matter. What the boys did, however, mattered a great deal. Well, I just want to let you know, even after all this time—I'm pretty okay myself." Many of us will simply say that we've always felt like we were a disappointment to those who counted most to us, that we could never measure up. Perhaps we quit trying, launched a career of compensatory overachievement, or pursued a goal that did not exist in the real world, such as gaining acceptance from someone who did not have it to give in the first place.

Some of us will undoubtedly tell stories of sexual or physical abuse when we had no ability to understand the crime committed against us other than "I must have deserved it." We may find the arrow in the heart was emotional abandonment: the nurturing people we needed just were not there. They were never home, or if home, they were drunk or totally preoccupied with other concerns. As a result, we came to think of ourselves as invisible, unimportant, uncared for.

Strangely, the tendency is to brush off major traumatic events from other people's childhoods. We quickly say, "Well, sure, you're depressed. Of course you're going to have major problems coping." How glibly we ignore the trauma with a small "t" that is ground zero for the traits that add up to our *own* DLS!

But it insults pain to suggest that we can arrange our lives in such a way as to appear that the hurt never happened. It *did* happen. It is our history. It is knit into our bones. In many cases, it is both the source of our greatest strengths as well as the dwelling of our ghosts and shadows. The goal is not to diminish the reality of that personal wounding, but to declare that these events need not doom the quality of the life we are living today.

Take the person, for example, who identifies with the desperate need for love. Most likely, he or she will also harbor a tremendous fear of intimacy. If that person can recognize that this fear is born of some long-ago imprint laid down by more events than could ever be remembered, the inevitable result will become clearer. These old patterns, notwithstanding all the hunger for love, predict adult relationships that are incapable of bringing emotional satisfaction. Of course such relationships will fail. That old message, emotional as well as cognitive, will inevitably be transmitted along the E-mail network. Everything is related.

What Do I Do Now?

The vital question, of course, is "What do I do now?" So what if we have some degree of understanding as to the nature of DLS? That doesn't relieve the pain one bit. What are we to *do* about it? The two action steps are simply "get set" and "go."

The first step of preparation is to realize that no one lives in a vacuum. Human beings do not function well alone; to isolate ourselves is to guarantee continuing depressive living syndrome. The irony is, however, that the more negative our patterns become, the more we tend to isolate. Thus, the work of conquering DLS is not to be attempted alone. Certainly, there is a part of this work that must be done separately; no one else can do it for us. But we cannot do it completely alone. The power of one is immense, but it is not as powerful as the power of one, plus one, plus one, plus one…plus The One that is God, as we understand God to be.

The ideal approach to the action steps is to visualize them taken in the context of "your team." Perhaps your team includes a professional, perhaps not. Many have found that seeking professional help, at least at the beginning of the journey, saves a lot of valuable time and energy.

Whatever fits, whatever we are able to do right now, is right. We just have to start. Once we begin, we won't be able to anticipate what doors will open—doors we never knew existed. Step by step, progress on the journey will not only become possible, it will become inevitable. Remember the man in the back seat of the big old car, leaning forward to encourage Peggy behind the wheel. Both of them were "trapped," but by working through their dark corners together, reaching toward each other, they found a way out. No one does it alone.

Get set

There are three steps involved in getting ready: committing, understanding, and establishing a structure.

Committing: Nothing happens without a decision. To decide is to begin. A decision today to run a marathon does not mean that we will run the marathon today, tomorrow, or next week. Life doesn't work that way. It means that today we make the decision to begin to get into shape so that when the time is right, we will be ready. The more conscious the decision, the more powerful the decision.

Several years ago, I happened to be in New York on the Sunday the huge New York City Marathon was run. Late in the day, the oldest finisher—a man well into his eighties—was being interviewed on television. Of course, the interviewer asked the man how he was able to run marathons at his age. How was he able to accomplish such a marvelous feat?

The man's answer contained the wisdom of the ages. He said

that at a certain point he simply started to "got ready." Some thirty years before he ran that marathon, he had suffered a heart attack. In failing health, he had no energy. He might have settled for that, he said, but eventually he got tired of having his children treat him like a fossil.

Who knows why that was enough to get this man motivated; conversion experiences are unpredictable and spiritual. Sometimes we create circumstances that are conducive to making the decision, and sometimes the decisions are made for us—often with our help, like eating fatty food, getting no exercise, and then having a heart attack. But when the light actually goes on, when the lamp flares to life, motivation moves in.

At some point, the light went on for this man. Then what? "One step at a time," he said. "At first, I could hardly get my running shoes on. I felt foolish." For a while, he would just sit still with his shoes on. That was his first step. Then he started to walk to the end of the block. Eventually, he could go around the block, and when that got to be routine, he was ready for progressively stronger wings.

You get the idea: from the house to the end of the block; from a block to a mile; from one mile to several miles; from several miles to a marathon. It all started with the decision to take that first step toward the front door. Even before that, actually, was the man's decision to buy a pair of running shoes.

"Of course, you have to keep at it," the man concluded. "Sometimes I had to run in the rain or deal with rude drivers. I had to put up with lots of side aches and minor pains. But it all amounted to putting one foot in front of the other."

This man's E-mail, flashing through his inner circuitry, began telling him, "You can do it." The fitter he became, the better he liked it and the more positive his E-mail became. It felt good.

The better it felt, the more he ran. The more attention and applause he received, the more committed he became. His E-mail became his best friend rather than his worst enemy.

"I can do things now that I couldn't do when I was thirty," he said. What an enviable place to be—and he got there one step at a time, literally.

Understanding: Remember the words of my friend in the London apartment: "If you understand how something works, you can probably fix it." So how does your E-mail work? What is the nature of your DLS? As you peel back the layers of your present reality and look at your inner workings, what do you see?

The patterns reviewed in Chapter 3 were meant to be a guide for telling your own story. Looking back now, use those guides to think through your own story. It may help to write it down in the following way:

- One of the traits I rated high on in the self-evaluations was… (See pages 46–53.)
- Given this trait as a starting point, and using the Cycle 1 triangle (page 67), what are my thought patterns (my recurring thoughts, such as anger)? What are my emotional patterns (how I usually feel, such as joylessness)? What are my behavioral patterns (my typical actions, such as indecision)?
- Referring to the Cycle 2 triangle (page 70), how do the consequences of this inner cycle affect my social life? my relationships? my "success" quotient?
- Referring to the Cycle 3 triangle (page 75), how do these consequences affect my mental patterns? my emotional patterns? my behavioral patterns?

Again, what is impossible to do at a given time, what seems to be just too much, is no doubt just that: too much. Many of us who struggle with depressive living syndrome are in such a state that any lengthy introspection, let alone writing project, is too much. If that's true, we can simply cut the project in half. We don't have to try to do it all. Perhaps we should just think about it first. Like the gentleman who learned to run the marathon one step at a time, perhaps we need to make a decision to write just one sentence a day. How hard can it be to jot down one sentence about our daily thoughts? If we just take a step back and observe our thoughts, detach from them, and watch ourselves thinking, we can examine what comes up.

Many have found some power of choice in just realizing what it is they are thinking. Until we take a step back and look, many of us have no idea what thoughts our spirit is chewing on. One step further along, however, and we begin to assume the power of decision. Perhaps we say, "Nope, that isn't good enough. I do not chose to live in the house those thoughts build."

Just for today then, we can commit ourselves to stepping back and writing a sentence or two about our typical thought patterns. As we "build up" our endurance, it may then become possible to see the connections between thoughts and feelings. We may very well see the E-mail of one cycle creating the E-mail of the other. Gradually, we may be able to see one triangle intersecting, causing, running alongside, feeding from and feeding into the second triangle. Slowly, we will begin to understand how our own story works. When we do, we will see the tracks that our train is running on.

Clearly, this process will be immeasurably aided if it is not attempted alone. We need to find someone we can share with. As difficult as this may be for those of us who have been isolated for years, we must try it. The very decision to allow someone into our inner sanctums is in itself a potent medicine in dispelling the dark veil of DLS. It is eye-opening to no longer be alone.

Slowly but surely, as we begin "getting set," we will get to know ourselves and the cycles within. From that point on, options will unfold that we've never thought possible.

Establishing a structure: At this point, we must decide how we are going to keep moving on a daily basis. In effect, how will we create a golden ladder to carry us up and out of the pit of depressive living? A structure is made of specific behaviors. Four criteria may be used to evaluate the kind of daily behaviors that make a difference.

First, the behavior must be *clear.* We must be clear and specific about what we think will start positive E-mail. If the behavior is not specific, it does not contribute to structure.

A commitment to "be good to myself" or "get in shape" or "do better," for example, is fine in general, but does not serve as a solid and reliable rung on that ladder, because it doesn't give us anything to stand on; it isn't specific enough. If there is no clear, specific behavior, then there is nothing to hang our commitment on; there is nothing clear to do or repeat.

Under "be good to myself," the specific behavior might be "tell myself three good things that I did today" or "name three marvelous personal qualities that are absolutely as true as any negative qualities that may describe me."

Rather than "get in shape," which is far too general, you might decide to walk for five minutes a day, or take five deep breaths twice a day. (No, five deep breaths is *not* silly. If it is a first step, then it is the first step toward successfully completing a marathon of some kind.)

Rather than the generality of "doing better," perhaps you can make a daily list of just two things you will accomplish. This is a thousand times better than having so many tasks swirling around in your head, like a tornado, that you don't get a thing done. Perhaps you could take the time to think of one thing you did each day and congratulate yourself on its completion.

Next, the behavior must be *doable* if it is to help keep us moving on a daily basis. Obviously, it makes no sense and does no good to commit to doing something we can't possibly do—at least not now. How many times have we done that? In the heat of some wellspring of good intentions, we may not only decide to get going, but to do it in a way that even Hercules could scarcely accomplish.

Where we are is where we are, and wherever we are is the best place to begin. Besides, where we are is not the point! What direction we are going is the point! All of life is process, a journey. The direction we are going—positive or negative—is infinitely more important than where we are at any given time. We will, sooner or later, arrive at the point we are moving toward if we choose to do what we can do. Anything more will hinder progress.

For example, it is not absurd to start a physical-health program by taking five deep breaths a day, if that is all that is possible. On the contrary, it is wonderful. It is marvelous because that behavior is pointing you in the right direction. It is getting salvation information via the E-mail circuit. Just looking in the mirror for ten seconds a day (after a lifetime of avoiding) and giving yourself a compliment can be as important as finishing a race in world-breaking time. Because, for you, it *is* world breaking. It is breaking out of the old world and starting to build a new one. You cannot live in a new reality until you get it built.

If you ask yourself to do an impossible thing, you simply need to cut it in half. If even that remains too difficult, you cut again. If you keep cutting until you reach a level of activity that *is* possible, you have made a tremendous start. Only what is doable will be of any value because that's all you can do. It's right for you, and when done again and again and again, it begins to program your E-mail circuits with positive data.

Next, the positive behavior must be *repeatable*. Most of the buzz on our E-mail circuits is habit—long practiced, deeply embedded habit. And habit, of course, is the result of repetition. The only way new habits can be formed is by the same process: repetition to the point of habit. That is why structure is so important. Structure is the critical discipline that creates the environment that promotes repetition.

Obviously, if the behavior around which a structure is to be built is not clear and doable, there is no chance for repetition. Something that can't be done even once can't be repeated. But once the behavior is both clear and doable, then we *do* it—and we do it again, and then again. Joyful living, like depressive living, is the result of experience that has been repeated until it becomes familiar. Once a pattern is familiar, a change is rarely considered until something, like reading this book, urges us to take a step back so we can see what is going on. Only then can we make a free, conscious, concrete decision. What will it be? Stay where we are or move to a "new address"? That becomes our choice.

How well I remember a lovely woman coming up to me after a seminar on DLS. She had a special "insider's question," as she put it. With a knowing wink she said, "I understand what you are saying. I understand my story, and I have already started my journey with clear, specific actions. I understand all this…" and here she gave me that knowing, just-between-us, head-tilted look.

"Now, what do I do next?" The implication was that she was not a novice, that she had been working on herself for a long time. She felt she had graduated to the "next level." She was implying that what I had just presented in the seminar was all well and good for beginners, but what about her? She was ready for something deeper—the "real stuff."

My answer was, no doubt, a disappointment. All I knew to say was, "Whatever you are doing, do it again—and then do it again—and again. Pretty soon you won't even remember what the old way was like."

It took the woman about three more tries to accept the fact that I had no "insider information" to offer; I had no "deeper stuff"; I had no tricks or shortcuts. I told her that even Michael Jordan once said, long after he had established himself as one of the best basketball players of all time, that he still went out and shot at least one hundred jump shots before each game. Jerry Rice, the leading pass catcher in all of National Football League history, is known to be the hardest worker in the league. If there are no shortcuts for the superstars, I suspect there are none for us.

Finally, our clear, doable, and repeated behavior must have *support* of some kind. The support theme cannot be overemphasized. Rather than merely entertaining the concept of community, however, let's ask ourselves a concrete question: *Who will be my support people?* Name them.

The idea is to get practical and concrete. As hard as it may be to get started, you have to write a list of the names of several people who could serve as your support team. That doesn't mean, of course, that you need someone "better" than you are. This plank in your rescue raft is not about humiliation, but the very opposite. It is about discovering that you *are* worth someone else's time, that you *are* loved and valued by others, that you *do not* need to spend your life in isolation.

You don't want to choose someone who has a need to control your life, however. Your true community cannot be abusive. Realize that some people act out their own DLS in the form of control, by dominating others, by taking away their right to make decisions. Obviously, such persons can be of no help to you and can do considerable harm.

At this point, many of us might be saying to ourselves, *Well, there simply is no such person or persons in my life.* I offer this: if there is no one today, there could be tomorrow!

It may be that the idea of actually reaching out for support and forming a community is beyond you just now. In that case, you can think about it, write about it, read books that motivate you to move out of your pain. When you read about the steps that other people have taken, you are inspired to look at your own potential. You can listen to audiotapes that could send some new E-mail into your circuitry.

To "get set" is to begin thinking of the necessity of support.

Go!

The moment of "go" can be divided into three parts: go inward, go outward, and go upward.

Going inward: This is soul work. It involves feeding the soul with information and motivation. As in all this work, we must be gentle with ourselves here. We do not want to take on more than makes sense.

For example, you might want to consider doing some daily reading. In the privacy of your own home, you can begin reading informational or motivational material for perhaps only three minutes a day–or less. You can always read more as you become more comfortable. You can take the time to find reading material that specifically lifts up your spirit; that may be Scripture, a favorite book of poetry, or one of the many fine "thought-for-the-day" books.

I know many people who have created a structure that allows them time every day to feed their soul with good reading. These people begin to create their own "book of wisdom." They collect passages from Scripture, favorite sayings, poems, snippets of counsel and comfort gleaned from any number of places, and they generate a resource of nurturing material that feeds their souls. They make their own book. Every time they come to their "care of the soul" time, they feast on what nourishes them most.

Audiotapes can also provide a rich means of going inward. In our day and age, there are countless sources of good information and motivation on audiotapes. You can listen to your spiritual food.

One afternoon, when I was walking across a parking lot on my way to the grocery store, a car slammed on its brakes right in front of me. As the driver's window slid down, I thought, *Oh boy, what's this. I don't think I cut anyone off when I pulled into the lot.* (Notice how automatic the negative E-mail starts flashing.) A cheerful voice shouted out of the car, "Listen!" Coming from the driver's tape deck was my own voice giving a taped inspirational talk. "I listen to you all day long," the man said. "It's easy, since I'm a salesman and drive around a lot." I'm sure he had many other tapes he listened to as well, but it was a treat to know that while I'm buying groceries, someone else is enjoying a tape I made long ago–and hopefully is growing stronger as a result.

We are what we think. Listening to motivating tapes can change the way we think and thus change the way we are and see the world. Any action taken to begin changing the way we think can be the lightning rod of our E-mail circuits.

Going outward: This is behavior taken in the outer world that begins to prove to us that "different" is possible. As with the inward journey, outward action is important because any success becomes a vital steppingstone on a completely new highway. Do not discount any action so taken; do not consider any success, no matter how small, as too insignificant to count. It all counts.

Possible outward steps may be as simple as going to the mailbox every day. If your DLS has you trapped in your house, you can choose (perhaps fortified by your reading or tapes) to spend just ten seconds walking to the mailbox every morning. Structure!

Far beneath your conscious mind, change will begin to happen. Deep within, you will begin to realize that if a walk to the mailbox is possible, then perhaps you can consider a walk to the end of the block. When that becomes possible, who knows: a marathon may be in the future.

Writing cards and letters to people is another simple outward behavior. It doesn't matter what or how much you write; it doesn't matter to whom you write. The important thing is to reach out, to get back in the game. Perhaps you can write to a relative you've lost touch with; perhaps your children, your parents, or a distant friend would appreciate just a word or two. Your note doesn't need to be a great literary work—just say hello, share a little news, and invite a response.

Making a commitment to do one letter or card a week is clear, doable, repeatable, and can be naturally supported with a response from the recipient. If you set a time to do this each week, you increase the odds of success to a point that no casino would tolerate.

Who knows what will happen with such contact. Everything is related to everything else. All of a sudden, someone may write back, expressing their tremendous appreciation for having heard from you, and what a powerful and positive impact that can have on your E-mail. Real and meaningful dialogue is sure to begin. The sour apple starts to become sweet.

Making physical contact with others is another outward behavior. Call a friend, a relative, a neighbor, and line up a luncheon or plan to go to a movie or a play. Call the editor of your local newspaper and make a comment. Write your congressperson about social policy that you want to comment about. With this kind of outreach, your E-mail starts to change in wondrous ways—ways that you never could or would arrange on your own, ways that could never be anticipated in a thousand years.

Here is a list of other simple, small, doable behaviors. Obviously, there is no comprehensive list of every possible get-going activity. These are but starters.

- Buy and read a magazine.
- Save a dollar.
- Open a savings account.
- Buy something nice—for yourself or someone else.
- Go to a movie.
- Smile at three people you ordinarily wouldn't.
- Write down three blessings you enjoyed today—do it every day.
- Voice one need to someone (a need that ordinarily you would "stuff").

- Ask for help at least once a day.
- Look up one new word in the dictionary each week.
- Do your best to make one person smile every day. (If he or she doesn't respond to your efforts, that isn't your fault. You will be making an honest attempt to get that lamp lit every day, with or without that person's response. Yours will burn brighter even if his or hers doesn't.)

We must start where we are. What may be easy for one of us is difficult for another. This is not a contest. The important thing is to get going in the right direction. For some of us, it may be behaviors such as those listed above. Others may have more task-oriented things to accomplish, like getting a résumé together, mailing it out, and making a follow-up phone call. Some of us may want to check out educational opportunities or begin developing a deeper, more personal relationship with someone. Perhaps we need to make a decision about a commitment or try to reconcile with a family member.

Once the ball starts rolling, there will be no stopping the forward rush. Our dark corners will be eliminated—at least to the degree that they were experienced before—and this is when the need for support becomes especially important. Remember that support involves regular meetings with those we have chosen to walk with us: our team. Like everything else in our lives, progress will be the result of "doing it" and not just "thinking it."

Perhaps you have to start with asking just one person to talk with you. You don't need to enter into deep conversations at first; friendly time together may be all you need. You might meet for a cup of tea or pie and coffee. You do what is doable—nothing more and nothing less.

Perhaps you're ready for a heroic step, like going to a self-help meeting—not a confrontation group, not a situation that makes you terribly uncomfortable. Rather, you venture into a gathering of fellow human beings who come together with a common need: a need to find some strength greater than any one has alone.

Perhaps for the first month—or even six months—you hardly say more than your name. Fine. You are there. You are voting with your feet. You show up. You can rest assured that change is happening. Deep within, healing is taking place. It may take some time for that healing to make itself felt, but the process is in motion.

Slowly, no matter how inconceivable it may seem now, you will find yourself bonding with one individual, several, or the whole group. You will feel yourself drawn to others. Then, with time, you become a valued group member. If you hang around long enough, you may even become an "old-timer." People will then start coming to *you* for the same kind of comfort, understanding, and rebirthing that you once sought. In their dear, hurt faces you will see your own. As you touch their hearts, you feel your own pulse beating. Why? Because not too far under the skin we are all the same person. We are all a part of the heart of humanity.

The presence of community and our appreciation for that support: there is no outward behavior that is more important. By connecting with our fellow human beings on the journeys, all the bases will be touched.

Going upward: The combined effects of inward and outward behavior will bear fruit, but not the full and abundant life that Jesus promised if we don't go *upward* as well. The word *upward* is a reference to prayer and meditation. "Conscious contact with

God as we understand God to be..." is the way one system of positive living puts it.

The more that DLS captures our spirit, the more difficult it is to experience a loving walk with a caring God. Under the crushing weight of all that DLS implies, our sense of spirituality is often a first casualty. Dark breeds dark, just as light breeds light. Whatever our sense of what or who God may be–whether that concept of God is caring or punishing–*any* reaching out in an open, honest attitude to a loving Higher Power works. It is especially critical to the work of reconnecting.

Nothing in science, nature, or psychology happens in a vacuum; everything is related to everything else. For decades, Alcoholics Anonymous has used the symbol of the camel. At first glance, it makes great sense; camels can go without a drink for days and days. Dry equals sober. Since AA is about sobriety, the camel makes sound symbolic sense. As obvious as that might be, however, there is a deeper meaning. The camel also begins and ends each day on its knees. So the deeper meaning of the symbol speaks to the importance of spirituality.

I wish I had the power to adequately put into words the following experience. This is the story of a person who has just begun to sense the presence of an all-loving, all-caring Reality: a God who is always there. I let his own words tell his story, as I share with you a letter he wrote.

> I cannot say exactly when my "recovery work" began. I sort of grew into it. After a lifetime of various spiritual and healing experiences (born again, a deeply religious adolescence, marriage encounter, charismatic renewal, inner healing, and so forth), I experienced a desolation and loss of belief after the death of my

son, Peter. That was eight years ago. Peter suffered the same chardiac abnormality that claimed the life of my first son, George.…

To make a long story short, over the ensuing years I became progressively more cynical and disillusioned with God and religion.…Slowly I realized that, though I was not "out of control," I was nonetheless behaving addictively toward religion, sex, people, depression, negativity, and my wife. My depressive behavior was making my life unhappy and damaging my relationships.

The marvel is, this man didn't quit. The magnetism between his God and his inner core would not permit it. He began to reach out.

I have been meditating to quiet music, consciously letting my woundedness take me where I need to go. I try to quiet the chatter of my left brain (from the lists in my notebook, it is evident I am very left-brained) and to allow my feelings to exist. As of yet, I have little faith in my Higher Power, but I am taking that on faith. I don't quite know what that means, but I am trying to remain open with respect to God.

This man goes on to mention other behaviors he started taking responsibility for in his quest for spiritual freedom. What makes me smile is his line about "…trying to remain open with respect to God." If he does, he will find that a torrent of liquid fire will flood through that opening.

God is many things, but surely high on the list is God as a totally committed, desperate parent searching for the lost child.

Have you seen the commitment of the parent of a lost child? That parent will move heaven and earth to find the child who has wandered off, and no one moves heaven and hell better than God. If this man, or any of us, leaves an opening, bet the farm God will be there. We don't have to be smart, tough, holy, beautiful, sinless. All we have to be is *there*, waiting with open arms, saying "Yes."

Sadly, however, our E-mail becomes fouled, and the light dims and gradually goes out. We quit waiting. Most of us don't deliberately turn our backs on God as we understand God to be; there's far too much blame and guilt in that scenario, and blame and guilt do not lighten a spirit. But we do lose God. Somewhere through the years, the E-mail becomes so cluttered and painful that we shut down to the one Reality that we most long for: God.

Whatever the past, however, *now* is what counts, as well as the future we are building out of this now. Right now we have a choice: we can chose upward behavior, a reaching out toward Life and Power, an opening of the perhaps long-rusted and blood-soaked hinges of our soul. That Power and Life are real, holding a healing light that longs to be let in.

No one can honestly say that the journey is easy—in spite of words like *light, power, hope, rebirth*, and *joy* that are used to describe it. Although these words carry strength, and what they represent is true, something else must be added to avoid unexpected frustration; something else is needed to confront the "sentries" that fight to maintain the status quo all along our E-mail routes. Without that something else, these loyal guardians will do their job relentlessly, making no distinction between helpful or harmful input, healthy or unhealthy input, friendly or unfriendly input. Their mission is to defend.

When we challenge the sentries by introducing radically new messages into our E-mail circuit, these "habit guardians" will respond with the energy and tenacity of white blood cells attacking what they sense to be hostile invaders in our blood. It's always a fight. When we begin to peel back the layers of dead feelings and old memories, there may well be a huge outpouring of guilt, grief, and anger. Many people speak of feeling overwhelming sadness for a while. *For a while*–that is the operative phrase; it won't last. The battle can be fierce, but the tide will turn, provided support and all the various activities of a program are used.

If and when the time comes, there are professional specialists who can assist us in dealing with the deep emotions that will surface throughout this process. This possibility should not worry us. By the time we need them, we will be strong enough and have enough support to do what we must do.

The prescription is simple: keep at it. The "insider information" that I offered the lady at the DLS seminar holds true for all of us: do it again and again and again. Believe it. Whatever we do, think, say, or feel often enough will gradually become normal, one step at a time. We will soon be so far along the road that we will scarcely imagine where we were when we started–and we will have arrived there without taking any great leaps. We simple took the steps we were able to take, one at a time.

One day we *will* arrive–not at the end, but at the beginning. We arrive when this particular walk in the sun is over. Whatever happens beyond the shade, happens. But for this part of the journey, how wonderful if we can smile with satisfaction and truthfully say that the ride was worth it! In the long run, so what if it wasn't easy. Just as long as we end up being glad we were here.

7

Goal-Setting:
Before It's Too Late

"People don't plan to fail. They fail to plan."

This pearl of wisdom is used by everyone from financial planners to career counselors. It is as true for us as it is for them. Even depressive living syndrome, for all its deeply personal and complicated causes and expressions, eventually yields to goal-setting.

The irony is, the deeper we are stuck in DLS, the less energy and spirit we have for anything so seemingly syrupy as goal-setting. Even mentioning goal-setting in the same breath as depressive living can seem like touting the advantages of marathon running to someone just recovering from heart surgery. But "seemingly so" doesn't make it so.

As repetitive negative E-mail flashes around our circuits, what becomes normal is the *experience* of frustrated failure. That is why we sink deeper into the mud: our experience tells us there is no use trying and there is no power available to make things any different. Experience is truth.

Chapter 6 outlined the components of a program that can produce experiences of success. This chapter highlights the fact that those of us trapped in DLS do not live our lives from the standpoint of planned outcomes. Most of us simply do tomorrow what we did yesterday. Why? Because we have no plan, no map, no new idea. As a result, we live reactive rather than proactive lives.

So if planning can make such a difference in life, why don't we plan? Because our negative E-mail constantly tells us, "Don't be stupid. Nothing is going to change. Life stinks; it always has and always will—at least for me." Trapped in that cycle, we experience life as failure.

But life does not have to be like this. Goal-setting, if done correctly—and we can do it correctly—makes sure it is not. Grant's experience provides us an inspiring example. The significant thing about Grant was not that he was a recovering alcoholic; he had been sober for nearly thirty years. And it wasn't especially significant that he was a successful car salesman; lots of people who have been stuck at their professions for many years have achieved a certain amount of financial success. No, the significant thing about Grant was something he *hadn't* done. As much as he applied the principles of goal-setting and successful living to his business life, worked on keeping a good attitude, never lost sight of service, and stayed willing to practice, practice, practice, he *never thought* of applying the same principles to his personal life. Somehow it just didn't occur to him.

As a result, Grant was not a happy person. In spite of the fact that he won state and national sales awards, he was desperately unhappy. There were too many loose ends—important things that had never been taken care of. His E-mail around business success was strong and healthy, but the circuitry around his personal life left him stranded in the wasteland of the Big Empty.

Grant came face to face with the Big Empty when his eighty-year-old mother was diagnosed with terminal cancer. As deep in Grant as deep goes, there was a painful gap between him and his mother, some unfinished business that symbolized most of what he felt his life was about. As in many alcoholic homes, there had been horrendous stress and strain in all his family relationships. But that was, supposedly, all played out long ago.

As his mother was letting go of life, however, Grant felt a different kind of ache, a deep wailing inside. It was not just that he wanted to mend fences with his mother before it was too late. Grant really wanted to create some link, some bond, that was never there in the first place. He wanted to tell his mother how much he loved her and how sorry he was for all the pain she had endured in her life. He wanted to tell her how important she was to him, and just perhaps, to hear from her that she loved him too. This, of course, is the stuff great literature is made of—the very heart of the heart of life. Neither Grant nor his mother, however, had the slightest skill to create this important eternal link.

While his mother's condition deteriorated, Grant decided to focus on one objective (which is what true goal-setting is: focusing on a single goal until it is obtained). This was how Grant made such success in the car business. Finally, he decided to make a success of his personal life.

In the presence of his support group, Grant made the commitment to take care of this important business. He set his goal. As with most goals, however, Grant's desired result was not immediately obtainable. If goals were that easy, there would be no need for goal-setting. We would achieve them as soon as we made them.

Shortly after making his commitment, Grant realized that some mighty obstacles stood between him and his goal—deep, personal, human obstacles, such as fear, shame, and guilt. The very newness of this kind of revelation began to loom as a major threat to Grant. Neither he nor his mother had ever attempted such a thing.

Goals are not real without plans. A goal without a plan is just a wish. Grant established his plan, and shared his plan with his support group. He told them how and when he was going to move toward his core goal. Every day he would spend some time with his mother, simply keeping her company. As a first step, this proved to be quite enough. Their usual modus operandi was *never* to talk about anything personal. Never get real.

By the end of the first week, Grant added to his plan. He decided to share just one "real" feeling with his mother. He would tell her how sorry he was that she was ill.

Now, to those of us who are skilled at such sharing, this may sound silly. Of course Grant should tell his mother how sorry he was that she was ill. But why didn't he tell her that he loved her? Why in the world wouldn't he just let it all out? Just talk!

Remember what has been noted many times: what is effortless for one person may be extremely awkward and stressful for another. This goal for Grant was terribly ambitious, perhaps impossible. It certainly was difficult enough that it would never have happened without goal-setting. If Grant didn't at least attempt to pursue this particular goal, the door of opportunity would soon be closed.

Grant focused on his goal and implemented his plan, and by the end of the week he and his mother began to tap into the realm of the personal. Grant's next step toward his goal was to come right out and tell his mother how much he loved her.

How easy to write those words! In truth, it was a monumental step for both Grant and his mother. Without a specific, concrete plan pointing him toward his goal, and without the "spinal starch" provided by his support group, Grant would never have done it. But he planned his work—and worked his plan.

Mere words can scarcely express the joy and wonder in Grant's face that week at his group meeting. He had arrived at the point where he could finally cross the bridge to his mother. Grant had told his mother that he loved her very much, and buoyed by her son's reaching out, his mother, in turn, had shared with him some truths that had been stitched in the depths of her soul for more than fifty years. Her soul was liberated.

After telling of his success, Grant quietly concluded, "Mother died last night." Who can doubt that the rest of Grant's life will be infinitely better for having set his goal and not missed this all-important "link." It is no small thing to make meaningful contact with a parent before it is too late.

Each successful advancement on his goal changed Grant's E-mail. Each step of the way provided a new experience upon which he could climb high enough to see the next hill, one effort at a time. Eventually, he not only saw the next hill, but the vast blue ocean beyond. This is how goals work. If we are to be freed from DLS, we have to achieve certain goals, either directly or indirectly. Directly is better, of course, and more efficient.

As we apply the following six-point plan for effective goal-setting to our own situation, we can expect a flood of negative E-mail. The mere exercise of thinking about goal-setting can set off a powerful chorus of noise in head and heart. But no matter; we must carry on. We are worth it. The quality of our life depends on it.

Goal-Setting Program

This exercise helps you develop your own goal-setting program. After carefully reading each section, reflect on your own unique set of circumstances, and write your responses on a separate sheet of paper.

1. Name your goal

Sit quietly and think about the challenge ahead of you. You are about to take the first steps toward changing your E-mail. Ask God, as you perceive God to be, to open your heart and mind, and to help you exercise self-honesty.

Make a list of two hundred things you would like to see, do, have, or become. Depressive living syndrome immediately says that this suggestion is impossible—simply because nothing *positive* is possible. It may seem a betrayal of your accustomed self to list even *five* desirable goals, let alone two hundred. It may seem an exercise of lunacy.

But exercise is just the point. Exercise begins to change your E-mail by introducing the *thought* of what would make your life freer, livelier, more enjoyable. It may take enormous courage to begin such a list, but freedom has always demanded courage. *See, do, have,* and *become.* Give it some thought right now. What accomplishments—even little ones—could create a "possibility experience" for you?

Some people might say "go back to school" or "take a trip to the ocean." Others might want to change jobs, rekindle a neglected friendship, improve their physical appearance (like losing weight, having their teeth fixed, or changing the color of their hair), become more patient, energetic, or risktaking. Whatever it is, the adventure of facing DLS begins with naming your goal. Put a name to some things you'd like to do or be. Give your dreams concrete form.

If you can't list two hundred items, list one hundred. If not one hundred, then fifty. If not fifty, then ten. If not ten, make a commitment to list three. Do what you can do, and then build on that. Deep inside, even if you list only three simple goals, you may be assured that a new ingredient has been added to the tired old E-mail circulating in your core.

You might structure your lists to look like this:

I WOULD LIKE TO SEE:

1.

2.

3.

4.

I WOULD LIKE TO DO:

1.

2.

3.

4.

I WOULD LIKE TO HAVE:

1.

2.

3.

4.

I WOULD LIKE TO BECOME:

1.

2.

3.

4.

2. Set your time line

Review your list and note how much time you think it will take to accomplish each goal. Next to those items that are obviously long-range goals, write how long you think it might take you to accomplish them: "two years," "five years," "ten years." Next to those items that can be accomplished in a shorter period of time, note how long you think it will take: "one-year," "three months," "six weeks."

Now review your short-range goals, the ones that you believe can be accomplished in less than a year. Select the one that means the most to you and focus on it. You are about to commit yourself to that goal: within one year you will create and accomplish a plan that will bring that goal into reality. And with that achievement, you will also experience the truth that you are, indeed, capable.

Expect resistance! Putting time frames around your goal is like beginning the exercise program you've talked about for years. You know what happens; as soon as you begin doing the exercise, your muscles start to rebel. That's what happens when rubber hits the road. It hurts—because it is getting real.

But without the strain, there is no strengthening of the muscles. So don't give up! Defy the fear and do it anyway.

3. Motivate, motivate, motivate

In real estate they say the important thing is location, location, location. In goal-setting, it's motivation, motivation, motivation. The motivation has to be stronger than all the reasons that previously kept you from achieving your goals.

So how do you motivate yourself? There are many ways, but try this: schedule time to clearly and completely write down what it will mean to you if you accomplish this goal. What will you gain? What is to be achieved or enjoyed? Why do you want to accomplish this goal?

If your goal is to lose weight, ask yourself *Why?* Do you want to feel better? Do you want to look better? Do you want to be healthier? Do you need to loose weight to take advantage of some other opportunity? On a much deeper level, you may simply want to prove to yourself that you *can* weigh whatever you want to weigh. Brainstorm; think it through. Take the time to make your goal something that is exciting to you—not just something you think you "should" do.

If your dream has been to see the ocean, ask yourself *Why?* Does the ocean have a special symbolic meaning for you? Is the trip just something you "always wanted to do"? Does it represent your freedom to "be an adult" and lead your life the way you choose?

Perhaps your goal is to find a support group or develop a comfortable and satisfying friendship. *Why?* What difference would that make in your life? How much good would it create? How will you be more of the person you want to be?

This kind of self-examination is an important part of the process of goal-setting. All too often we operate with no clear idea of why we do or don't do something. We leave most of our positive ideas wispy, unexamined, and up in the air. But to take charge of our life is the opposite of being pushed down the road by DLS.

Initiating change can be a most thrilling exercise, but you must tell yourself the truth. Dig deep. When you hit the chorus of ghosts and the shadows of doubt—just *do it*. Walk on through. Nothing can hurt you or stop you if you do not give it permission. Why *shouldn't* you have or be whatever it is you have selected from your short-range list?

Why? The question is critical, and the answer is the basic substance of motivation that you will draw on when doubt haunts your efforts. Spread the benefit out in front of you like a fur rug before the fireplace on a cold winter's night. Then wrap yourself in it.

4. Calculate your loss

This step is the reverse of Step 3. Now you will clarify for yourself what you will lose or miss if you allow your goal to go unclaimed. After all, that too is a choice. Either you benefit from its accomplishment or live without its fulfillment: those are your choices. The choice belongs to you because the power belongs to you. And as long as the power *is,* your DLS *is not.*

Think about the eighty-year-old gentleman who conditioned himself to run the marathon. What would he have missed had he let the negative E-mail win? What would life have been like for him if he had simply abandoned himself to slipping into deeper impairment? Of course, there was a price to be paid for his achievement, but the price of giving up would have taken a far greater toll.

Had Grant let "business as usual" be his guide, he would have missed a precious moment of healing with his mother. He realized not only the grace of making contact with his mother before she died, but the personal dignity and validation in *not* missing this connection.

The failure to examine what you have to lose is just as costly as the failure to examine what there is to gain. So often our wishful nonthinking is, *If I don't think about it, it isn't.* Somehow it doesn't exist. But your subconscious knows. Beneath normal, routine conscious thought, an accounting is continually taking place. With every rejection of what could be, you pitch a bit of negativity into the E-mail that leads to and adds up to DLS. If you never really look, you abdicate much of your ability to choose.

Once you have written what you stand to lose, you are in a position to ask yourself a few tough questions: *Am I prepared to lose this forever? Am I prepared to hobble down the road when I could just as well walk, smelling the flowers and enjoying the view of brilliant sky and rolling hills?* It's your choice—but what is the choice about? What is the "this or that"?

5. Select a partner

Goals that are not written remain mere ideas; they do not become goals until they are written. And goals that are not shared with a "trusted other" most likely will fall victim to the first negative breeze. Which one of us has not set a goal of some kind, not told anyone, and then quit—convincing ourselves it wasn't worth the effort, or it wasn't possible. When DLS came knocking, we said, "Come right in."

This "trusted other" is crucial. That person keeps you accountable. The very act of trusting another enough to share your goals is in itself a giant step away from DLS.

6. Just do it

Plan the work so you can work the plan. Think about how you could break your goal down into manageable parts. There is considerable wisdom in the saying that the best way to eat an elephant is one mouthful at a time. If your goal is to be achieved, there must be markers. How else can you tell if you're on target?

Where must you be six months down the line to be in a position to go further?

If you find that your time frame is off, fine. Most things take longer than we initially think they will or should. (Have you ever remodeled a kitchen?) No one knows why—they just do. So if your time frame is off, change it, not the goal. Talking with your "trusted other" helps you get a realistic fix on time frames.

If your goal is to go back to school, your plan may look like this:

> By the end of the first month, I will have selected five places that offer the courses I am interested in. By the end of the second month, I will have talked to people in the admissions offices at all five places. I'll scout them out and see which one fits me best. But suppose by the end of the third month, I'm still checking them out? Something came up during the second month and I didn't get to it. That isn't the end of anything. I simply have to push on to check out my options; that's *still* the next step. By the end of the fourth month, I will have selected the school I will attend, and I will be looking at class schedules. I will find out when classes are held, how many credits I will take, and what the costs are. By the end of the fifth month, I will have an application submitted. By that time I will have decided what classes fit my needs and interest, and what I can handle. By the end of the sixth month, I will be doing homework!

Try this process yourself; plan your work and work the plan. Take plenty of time to think through the details of your plan, and to share those details with your "trusted other." Write your own plan, being specific and including all relevant details, using the following model:

- Six months from now I will have accomplished...
- To be on target for that goal, *this week* I need to...
- To be on target for this week, *today* I need to...

The idea is not to kill yourself with pressure, but to ground your plan with specifics. You want to give your goal every possible chance of being accomplished, so you want to be concrete and realistic. If the time frame is too stringent, loosen it–but keep on track. When the going gets tough, remind yourself that *you* chose the goal because of what *you* have to gain and what *you* have to lose.

Do whatever it takes to remain strong, focused, motivated, and encouraged. Keep your goal in front of your mind's eye. Many put up "goal boards" with pictures that represent their goals. Focus means single-mindedness. If your mind is focused on the accomplishment of an exciting goal, the negativity that is at the heart of DLS gets crowded out; there isn't room for both. Do whatever it takes–inspirational tapes, books, change of friends, beginning to attend meetings or educational events. The escape route from DLS is a one-step-at-a-time proposition.

This chapter began with a slogan: "People don't plan to fail. They fail to plan." Another slogan is equally on target: "Successful people are simply those who are willing to do what others aren't." Define your own success–having more fun, being sober, losing weight, getting a better education, acquiring more patience. Whatever it is, it takes effort, especially when obstacles arise–and there are always obstacles in the way of any success. Some people are willing to make the effort and others are not. People who are successful are not those with the most talent, not those with the "right breeding," not those who are most intelligent. People who succeed are simply those who are willing to do what it takes–over and over and over again until the hill is finally theirs.

Beating DLS is of supreme importance. It is perhaps life's greatest success. For no matter what else you accomplish, if you have not enjoyed life, what have you done? In the struggle against DLS, certain things are required. Perhaps those requirements are not exactly the same for everyone, but all require consistent effort. For some it may be finding a qualified doctor and getting appropriate medication–then sticking with it. For others it may be finding a positive, strong support group–and sticking with it. Some people may need to begin by reading and listening to messages that contradict their constant negative E-mail that says, "No, you can't!" Whatever it is, movement must be made. Some people will be willing to make the effort–be successful–and others won't.

At first, goal-setting may seem ephemeral, cutesy, "new age," or "positive-thinking" nonsense. But nothing could be further from the truth. Time after time studies show the common denominator among people who have achieved great things: they knew what they wanted and went after it with dogged determination. Their determination was translated into a concrete, specific plan that could be modified, checked, graded. If you don't know where you want to go, you will wind up somewhere else.

A Critical Overview

Recall the life scenarios in Chapter 2, where we looked at the roots and the fruits of eight personal life stories. With careful attention, reread Cynthia's (page 27) and Bill's (page 29) scenarios. Now that we have a better understanding of the patterns and cycles at work in DLS, a study of their stories will allow us to look at goal-setting in the light of real-life situations and to nail down the principles of this book.

There is, after all, a reason for each of these chapters and the order in which they appear. Goal-setting has everything to do with understanding your own life scenario (Chapter 2). Your own scenario caused the patterns you have established (Chapter 3) and the negative E-mail running rampant through our mind (Chapter 4). The wounds caused by your negative E-mail resulting in DLS create a horrible emptiness in the center of your heart that, in turn, creates even worse conditions (Chapter 5). If you are to recover from those wounds, there must be healing (Chapter 6), and a key ingredient of healing is goal-setting (Chapter 7). You will soon see how this process is greatly enhanced and enriched if done in the context of spirituality (Chapter 8).

So how might goal-setting make a difference to Cynthia and Bill? A study of their respective goals, motivations, losses, support systems, and plans will demonstrate how potentially successful they will be. Such a study will assist you with your own goal-setting.

Cynthia

A large girl born into a family that valued males, Cynthia came to see herself as unacceptable, flawed, and unlovable. The worse she felt, the more she ate–which made her feel worse, which drove her to eat. She learned to hide behind her feelings of inadequacy by refusing to take responsibility; she played dumb and inept. The less she understood, the less responsible she was for making decisions. The more she played out this self-defeating cycle, of course, the worse she felt about herself.

Goal-setting: Cynthia made her list of goals, and then narrowed that list to focus on feeling better about herself: to stop hiding, to come to accept her body type without justification or shame. But Cynthia knew that body type was not the only contributing factor to her size; she knew that she was overweight. She determined to bring her weight down by one dress size. She had many other things on her list as well, of course, but this was the most important one to her.

When: When Cynthia separated her feelings from her thoughts, she knew that the timing around becoming more assertive and taking responsibility for her weight and looks was well within her control. The beginning of this liberating process could take place immediately.

Why: Cynthia took her time to get as deeply into herself as she could. She "did what it takes" to figure out why it was important to her to step out of her own shadow. She realized that there was much to gain: her whole life. Why *shouldn't* she learn to feel good about herself? She wasn't a bad person. Regardless of what others thought or said about her, why should she give *them* her power? No! She was who she was, and that "who" was good. And if she decided to change, she could be the person she decided to be.

Loss: Cynthia took equal time to clarify what she stood to lose if she denied her own journey. She didn't like the quality of her life. DLS ruled her every waking moment (as well as her sleeping moments—she just wasn't as aware of it). She decided that too much of her life was a waste. To live the way she did, when she had many opportunities that are denied others, was just a terrible waste. She was determined not to live her life with the "weight" of the world on her heart.

Sharing: It took great courage, but Cynthia identified a trust-worthy friend, took a risk, and shared her goals with that person. She asked her friend to walk with her and hold her accountable—perhaps to hold her physically at times as well. Cynthia knew that she would become discouraged now and then, that her courage would dip. So she asked her friend to be there for her, to offer encouragement when she needed it, and to push her when necessary. She knew she couldn't do what she wanted to do if she tried to accomplish it alone.

The plan: Cynthia committed herself to losing twenty pounds within a year. Less measurable but just as important, she also committed to being well past the automatic response of running from responsibility. She was not going to play dumb any longer.

Cynthia's first step was to find an aerobics class within a week, and to identify a weight-loss program she was comfortable with. By the end of the second week, she was going to be in action with both her exercise and weight programs. Regarding her learned fear of responsibility, Cynthia decided to *practice.* She made a commitment to, at least once a day, voice one opinion that ordinarily she would have concealed: an opinion about the weather, a political view, a current clothing fashion. *What* the opinion was didn't matter; voicing it did. Her E-mail changed.

Cynthia kept a daily log of her accomplishments, remaining aware of both pluses and minuses. At the end of the fourth week, Cynthia had increased her exercise sessions and was beginning to believe that she did not need certain kinds of food to feel good—or more to the point, to hide behind. She became ever more comfortable voicing her opinions, and gradually she could confidently say, "I can do that. I'll take care of that."

Slowly, the DLS fog began to lift from Cynthia's life. Although the road was not an easy downhill roll, Cynthia frequently consulted with her friend, planned the work, and worked the plan.

Bill

"No one will ever be there for you." This was the lesson Bill learned early in life. He learned to be "tough," to kill his feelings. In response, Bill became conditioned to never show a soft, approachable, or vulnerable side to others—even his four-year-old son. Of course, he wanted more emotional connection with his son; he just couldn't provide it.

Goal-setting: Bill had everything that mattered to him—except what he wanted most: to share in the "human" side of life and provide a more balanced emotional foundation for his son. On his list of what he wanted, he wrote things like "to hug my son for no reason," "to tell my son what is right with him at least as much as I point out what is wrong." Bill wanted to be able to sit on a park bench with his son and just have a good time, to laugh with him, to enjoy him and let him know that. "I want my son to not be afraid of me."

When: Bill understood that he could start to accomplish these goals at any time; there was nothing standing in his way but shadows. He simply had to get the lamp to work—and he could fix it. His DLS was the result of habits, and habits are learned by practice. But *any* habit can be learned. It's just a matter of what a person chooses to practice—and what a person chooses to keep practicing. Bill wanted to start practicing immediately.

Why: Bill took time to examine his motives; what was to be gained from this goal? He found that his reasons were tied around the very core of his life. He wanted more for his son. For himself, he wanted to know the happy, nurturing side of life that he could only guess at. When he saw family pictures in magazines or pre-views about movies with a father-son focus, the Big Empty inside of him would quiver.

When he took the time to reflect, Bill could envision the effects of his work filtering through the years to come. If he could give his son a better foundation, then that little boy could gift his son one day. Bill saw children yet unborn benefiting from all the efforts he could make to dispel his DLS.

Loss: How could Bill put his loss into words? What he had to lose was the dearest dream of his life—and he simply was not willing to live without it.

Sharing: The long-obeyed orders to "tough it out" and "do it on your own" made it extremely difficult for Bill to ask anyone for help. He knew, however, that if he wanted to reach his goal—if he wanted a happy, nurturing relationship with his son—he had to reach out and share; it just had to be done. As a businessman he knew that control of objectives was essential for success. Such control could only be had by building in accountability and sticking to a plan. It made sense.

Bill identified who his partner would be, and made his commitment to that person. The two met on a regular basis to review Bill's plan and to acknowledge his progress.

The plan: Bill made a commitment to say one "understanding statement" a day. Where perhaps others were *too* understanding, always making excuses, Bill had always been the opposite. He never noticed or gave any significance to the human element of life. As part of his plan, he would tell someone—on a daily basis—"That must be difficult" or "Good for you to keep at it" or "Tell me how you feel about this."

Bill slowly deepened his commitment to the terribly difficult challenge of touch. As he made himself pat others on the shoulder, he gradually became conscious of the power of touch. On a daily basis he practiced these skills with his son. Rather than pushing the child in a direction Bill thought was important, Bill asked the boy if *he* wanted to do a certain activity—or not. By dogged practice, Bill learned to ask if his son was tired or wanted to do something else. He stopped punishing the child when he cried and began encouraging him regularly.

Almost imperceptibly, Bill's E-mail began to change in a permanent manner. He was not only turning into a more humane person, but was actually becoming thoughtful and considerate as well. He began to realize the payoff when he started sharing in some precious moments with his son. These quiet, long-sought moments were more than just the presence of love; after all, Bill's father had loved him. Rather, they were the *experience* of love. For Bill, love had finally found its way across the bridge to another person. And with that crossing, DLS was left behind.

What goals would lift up *your* heart? Think about it. Then apply the program to *your* life. Be especially thorough with "why" and "loss." Keep asking yourself the key questions: *What will I gain? What will I lose?* The choice—and the power—are yours for the claiming.

8

Prayer and Depressive Living Syndrome: God Can Do What You Can't

The relationship between prayer and depression is similar to the relationship between sunlight and darkness. Think about it. We are able to embrace God only with the clarity of soul and vision of heart that our inner search has allowed.

With how much energy have we begun that inner search? Are we ready to stop defining ourselves by our brokenness? Are we willing to walk with this God who has revealed himself in the whispering breeze, in the crops ripe for the harvest, and in his Son, Jesus, who has come to walk with us?

Consider the following five "moments" of prayer as you get started on your journey. How does each relate to your life? As you read, keep in mind that every prayer that soars to God on eagles' wings tells you more of the eagle. Every prayer that reveals more of the eagle enables it to fly higher into the endless vastness that is God.

- The *prayer of quiet*, whose main element is reflection and whose main fruit is presence.
- The *prayer of listening*, whose main element is surrender and whose main fruit is peace.
- The *prayer of others*, whose main element is sharing and whose main fruit is trust.
- The *prayer of acceptance*, whose main element is seeking and whose main fruit is serenity.
- The *prayer of ministry*, whose main element is doing and whose main fruit is fullness of heart.

Prayer of Quiet

This is the prayer whose main element is reflection and whose main fruit is presence. For these two dynamics to harmonize, we must be receptive.

There is a difference between being passive and being receptive. Being passive means "laying back, with zero enthusiasm and energy." It means giving ourselves over to being "done unto" without making a conscious decision about what is happening in or around us.

Being receptive, on the other hand, is the state of being actively open to what is around and within us. It presupposes the beautiful quality of anticipation. As pray-ers, we are in touch with a mighty hymn rising up out of creation, and we want to be whole enough and present enough to hear it. Herman Melville gives us an image of this in his eerie work, *Billy Budd*, when he describes the demon and the angel as huge shapes gliding back and forth just under the surface of the ocean. It is not such a great leap to imagine ourselves as that ocean. A greater awareness of who we are and who God is glides unrealized just beneath our conscious grasp. Receptivity is the openness and the willingness to allow these nebulous shapes to take concrete form that we may see and know them. We do this in the state of reflection.

For some reason we often have the idea that praying is *talking*. Many of us feel our most authentic prayer is accomplished when we are filling the mental and physical airwaves with vibrations of one kind or another. But the prayer of quiet is something other than that.

The point of becoming receptive is to allow the universe to reveal itself—and what is that revelation but the constant summoning of our deeper selves to "come in" and "be seen." The prayer of quiet allows us to embrace those shapes gliding back and forth within us.

Quietness sets the stage for reflection. The prayer of quiet allows us to hear the messages that surround us at any given moment. That revealed "word" can then lead us gently both within and without.

Countless spiritual writers have encouraged their readers to look around. Jesus so often spoke of things like the birds of the air, the flowers blooming on the hillside, the fields of grain ready for harvest. To him, all creation spoke of the Father's presence. It is not different for us.

The rhythm of reflection and the prayer of quiet

I am reminded of a swimming party I attended some years ago. The party guests were residents of an institute for young adults who are physically challenged. In that setting, the messages to be heard (being receptive) in the prayer of quiet were almost deafening.

Being receptive: Anyone who has made a habit of the prayer of quiet will find reflection on wheelchairs to be a powerful meditation. The locker room we used at the pool party was narrow; two chairs could not possibly pass at the same time. When one resident was changing into his or her bathing suit, someone else had to wait for an aisle to clear before going on to the pool. It was stiflingly hot in that locker room; there was nothing anyone could do to improve the situation.

Reflection and prayer: Think about the hard reality of living in a wheelchair. So much of the essence of "finding" God lies in our acknowledgment that we need him—which includes the admission of our own powerlessness. So often we attempt to deal with our own anger, depression, or violence by ourselves. If God wants to come along, fine—but the journey is not fueled by his power; we insist on commanding the steering wheel.

Just a glance at the magnificent patience of those swimmers who were physically challenged, and their acceptance of powerlessness, spoke eloquently of our need to let go and to let God in. None of them ever expected life to be easy. But at that party, it wasn't even easy to sit and wait in that steaming room. Yet the Word was there.

Being receptive: One of the swimmers who could not hear was a lovely young woman who enjoyed the outing with the glee of a freed seal. To listen to her was to know her happiness. Frank, one of the aides of the institution, glided her back and forth in her innertube. Not knowing she could not hear, I asked Frank about the woman's speech. His beautiful response was, "Mary cannot hear, you see. You have to look into her eyes to see what she is saying."

Reflection and prayer: The main element of the prayer of quiet is reflection. If we were to quietly, receptively reflect on Frank's response, we would indeed know much of ourselves and God. *"You have to look into her eyes to see what she is saying."* To a lesser degree, is that not true of us all?

Just think of the missed communications among us: held back words, words not truly said, words deliberately misunderstood, words that fall short of the mark, words that confuse rather than clarify. Perhaps if we listened more with our eyes than with our ears, we would hear much more.

———

Being receptive: After I heard Frank's wise comment, I watched him. He *did* look into Mary's eyes, searching with gentle openness. Obviously, he truly wanted to "hear" what Mary had to say. He was receptive to her as a person.

Reflection and prayer: Prayer and praying are not always the same. At times a prayer can be a place to hide, a way to actually block off receptivity and listening. The gliding shapes remain hidden.

Frank's attitude and actions remind us of what praying *should* be. Are we not safe in the hands of God as Mary was in Frank's? Are we in less need of being held up? Are we somehow more capable of saving ourselves? Do we not, as desperately as Mary, need and want to be heard with the same loving concern that Frank heard her?

The humbling, startling fact is that we *are* in need; we are powerless; we are desperate to be held and heard with loving concern. Just as Frank was receptive toward Mary, we can know the intimate attention of God by deepening our receptivity through the prayer of quiet. God is looking in our eyes, listening to our hearts, speaking to us in the same subtle and overt ways that Frank used to communicate with Mary.

The prayer of quiet often teaches us that things are never what they seem. At that long-ago swim party, a group of us simply came to help some who couldn't swim on their own enjoy the water. Who would have thought we would be given a revelation of the loving God?

———

Being receptive: Debby was another aide from the institute. A natural-born gift-giver, Debby truly loved the young people in her care. She was not afraid of them or of herself. She knew that all young people love to "horse around" at swimming parties. It was no different there; Debby was right in the middle of the play along with everyone else. Her actions spoke out clearly: "Hey, you're all okay with me. We'll have a good time."

Reflection and prayer: When dealing with people who are physically challenged, there is a tendency to see *handicapped* people rather than *people* who have a physical challenge. The people at that swimming party were young adults, no different from other young people. Their needs, fears, joys, and pains were the same.

Handicapped is a strange word. For some reason we think it is a snap to decide who has a handicap and who doesn't. Yet people with physical challenges seem to have an advantage over people who do not: people who are physically challenged admit their limitations. Yet we're *all* "handicapped"! There are countless handicapping conditions that aren't signaled by obvious indications such as wheelchairs.

Reflection on Debby's attitude and presence reveals a telling sense of the presence of God with all people, although our own fears and lack of courage often block that presence. We tend to sculpt an image of God so far removed from scriptural revelation that there's no resemblance. Sometimes we may think, in our moments of deep despair, that God's presence is impossible for us. How, then, can we allow that loving Father's entrance?

It might be that many guests at the swimming party didn't think they deserved Debby's lavish, gentle, loving attention and gift-sharing. But how can they deny the reality of it when they see, hear, and feel it happening? Such presence cannot be faked.

Since so much of depressive living syndrome is rooted in repressed anger and loss of self-esteem, our ability to accept God's embrace becomes severely limited. In our own eyes, we become "handicapped," as well as "crippled."

So is there no hope? Is it true that others could not possibly embrace us if they "knew" us, if they looked into our eyes and "heard" what we long to say?

Beside the swimming pool and in the locker room, the voice of God was clearly saying to all who would hear: "Do you see how this girl loves and cares and plays? Do you see how no obstacle inhibits her loving concern? Then so shall I be with you, if you but let me. If you will be touched, I will touch." Mixing with the splash and laughter, that was the voice of unconditional love that could be heard in the prayer of quiet.

We can also hear the eloquent "scripture of nature" speaking to us in the prayer of quiet. Perhaps there is no phrase that occurs more frequently in theology than "death to life." How often we are reminded that Jesus died so we might live, that he hung on the cross so all of us could pass through the door of death and into new life. In fact, our Judeo-Christian tradition is rooted in the "death-to-life" exodus of the ancient Hebrews as they passed out of slavery into the freedom of the Promised Land.

I am reminded of the growing cycle of the potato plants. When they begin to bloom, giant water sprinklers provide the moisture needed to turn the plants deep green. When the weather is especially hot, the mist blowing off these irrigation machines above the green fields might make us think of Eden as it has been described for us by the sacred writers.

Within a few weeks after the potato plants blossom, planes dust the crops, killing the upward growth. This allows the potato, which is a root, to grow to its largest potential. Then comes the harvest.

The prayer of quiet; the prayer of reflection. We are like the potato plants: death to life. But unless fear, anger, unnamed hostility, and the refusal to trust another are "dusted" and killed, like the potato blossoms, there can be no life. Without death, the crop cannot be harvested, for there will be nothing to harvest.

We all meet trouble and tragedy in our lives: events and situations that often appear with a power beyond our ability to control. Perhaps it is sickness, lack of work, or an accident. Some of us might call it just plain bad luck—and maybe it is. But, like the crop being dusted, these events can be the touch of death from which life springs.

If you were to put this book down right now and look quietly and receptively around you, what voice might you hear? The tick of a clock speaking of time? the fragrance of a flower speaking of graciousness? the memory of a departed loved one speaking of mortality? the sounds of children speaking of life?

Prayer of Listening

This is the prayer whose main element is surrender and whose main fruit is peace. Praying by listening presupposes, of course, that someone is saying something; we can't listen to what is not being said. God speaks to us. Our task is to hear.

To give us a better chance to hear, God speaks to us in many ways. One of the most powerful ways is through Scripture. The prayer of quiet entails silent reflection on the powerful messages of God all around us. The prayer of listening is not only reflection but *surrender* to the Word of God given us in the Bible. Obviously, then, to hear God, we have to listen: we have to read the Bible.

Listening to the Word

It may be useful to clarify the word *read*. Have you ever noticed how many ways we read the printed or written Word? What is revealed largely depends on how and why we read.

When one of our teenagers was preparing for her driver's license test, she intently read the driver's manual. She didn't care who wrote the book or what the author might be saying between the lines. She simply wanted to know facts that would prepare her for the exam that would allow her to get a license that would permit her drive. That was all she cared about.

A friend of hers, on the other hand, was deeply interested in motorcar racing. He read everything available about the building and care of racing cars. He read about experts in the field and was thoroughly, personally, involved in all he read. He wasn't merely seeking objective answers to questions.

Then there's the lovers at the gift shop musing over the greeting cards depicting moments of love. They read with passion, tenderness, and play. He reads one, shows it to her, and they nod at each other as if to say, "Yes, I know what this means." Then she reads a card to him, and the "dance" repeats itself.

The lovers aren't reading for answers; they aren't reading articles about an interesting sport. Their reading is something else. Reading words of love is not quite like anything else. This kind of reading involves a giving and a taking—and a savoring of both. The *whole* person is involved. Love letters don't tell us *how* to love; they don't prepare us to pass a test. They reach into our hearts with love, and we respond with love.

Written words can be translated into totally different messages, depending on the translator. When an English teacher examines a love letter for spelling and punctuation errors, the letter ceases to be a love letter. It becomes something else, and in that process, its message is lost.

Scripture as a love letter

People read Scripture in many different ways, for many different reasons. Some read it to find "proof" that their point of view is right and that another is wrong. Interpreting the words to fit their own meaning, these people read to justify their prejudiced hearts. Others read Scripture as a historical document or as a moral blueprint for correct behavior.

Let someone else argue about the rightness or wrongness of any of these reasons for reading the Bible. The point is, Scripture is a love letter: the passionate words of a perfect Lover try-ing to communicate with us, the often contrary beloved.

This is not to say that there is no room or need for scriptural knowledge; obviously there is. The average person certainly needs to be somewhat familiar with the historical context of any given biblical text, the literary forms that were employed in the writ-ing, and the symbols and myths that are used to embody time-less wisdom. Lacking this knowledge, Bible study can become nothing more than a subjective way of talking to ourselves. All we hear are our own shadowy words.

Knowledge is only a small part of the experience, however; it does not replace love. The reading of Scripture must never be removed from the context of God inviting us into a loving rela-tionship. Knowledge is only an aid that helps us understand the passion, mystery, and timelessness of that invitation.

Scripture, existing in the realm of love, demands the surren-der of the heart to the One who calls. Any section of Scripture read in this light draws us closer to ourselves and to God. Peace begins to pervade our existence only when this surrender begins.

I recently attended the funeral of a man who could best be described as a wonderful "character." He marched to his own tune and sang his own song throughout his life. As his daughter said, "He gave God a run for his money." But God has far more "money" than any one of us could ever "run."

The theme of the funeral homily was based on John 6: 37-40:

> Everything that the Father gives me will come to me, and anyone who comes to me I will never drive away; for I have come down from heaven, not to do my own will, but the will of him who sent me. And this is the will of him who sent me, that I should lose

> nothing of all that he has given me, but raise it up on
> the last day. This is, indeed, the will of my Father,
> that all who see the Son and believe in him may have
> eternal life: and I will raise them up on the last day.

When read with eyes of love, these beautiful lines call forth a willing surrender. Such a response is natural because this verse paints such a beautiful, welcoming image of God.

The homilist for this man's funeral mass pointed out that most people have a "straight" and "proper" image of God. He suggested that if God were to walk into the church just then, most people would expect to see a figure that fit their own perceived image of God: a human form dressed in well-tailored, contemporary clothes, and most assuredly male. In a word, God's appearance would be "proper."

Yet there we were, burying Bill, a man who never concerned himself with what was "proper." When Bill retired from his painting job some years earlier, for example, the company he worked for asked him to have his picture taken with the other retirees. Of course he was asked to "dress proper." That meant a suit and tie, although Bill seldom wore such clothes. Neither had the others, for that matter. When the group gathered for the picture, there was one "character" who showed up wearing his white, paint-splattered bib overalls: Bill. That was the song he heard, and that was the beat he marched to.

"Everything that the Father gives me will come to me." Does God understand "characters"? Does God understand about retirement pictures and white bib overalls? Does God's love letter speak to the "characters" among us, or just to those of us who are "proper"? When Jesus spoke to the crowds, there must have been "characters" present. Just look at the apostles—and he loved them all. He did, indeed, understand. So many gospel stories depict people who would never show up for a picture in their Sabbath best. They would come as they were, and enjoy doing so.

Clearly, reflection on Scripture with an open, honest mind brings to light a face of God we never before recognized. How does that work? As *who we are* develops, so does our vision.

Ritualizing death for a Christian, as we were doing at Bill's funeral, weds the two concepts of finite humanity and "going back to God." Yet I suspect that we dress up the deceased person in our minds so that he or she is "proper" enough to make the trip. In the process we strip the person of all the character qualities that made him or her real in this life! Why? Perhaps it is because of the "proper" image we have of God. How could a totally "noncharacter" kind of reality ever understand some of the zany antics that make humans lovable?

Our thirst for intimacy

Reflect for a moment on Jesus "breaking the bread of his body." If it is true that destructive behavior in its many forms is a result of a lack of genuine intimacy, then Scripture meditation is for all of us. Again, it must be read with the eyes of love.

Whether we're aware of it or not, we all desire intimacy or closeness more than anything. But what *is* this closeness? What is it made of? How does it come about? What does God in Christ have to tell us or teach us about this crucial element of human wholeness?

Sometimes we tend to think of closeness as a "thing" that tantalizes yet eludes us, something we can see and objectify. But closeness is the name of an exchange more than a "thing." The nature of the exchange can be seen in a summer rain: the rain simply *falls*. It doesn't safely and deliberately pick its way to its final point of impact on the surface of the earth. It doesn't check to see if all below is safe or not. Rather, the rain falls freely and with vitality. And in this random impact, the grass becomes green, the fields ripen, the air is swept clean. So which part of this process is due to the rain and which to the earth? Where does one stop and the other begin? Is the freshness and greenness of the grass to be attributed to rain or soil? The truth? It is due to both. An exchange has been made. The openness of the earth receives the vitality of the rain.

We make human exchanges in the same way. Fear, anger, depression, alienation—all these conditions stand as obstacles to closeness. All come into being from our inability to exchange trust for trust, risk for risk. Fear and frustration are the afterpains of locked gates. In a human exchange, gate by gate and layer by layer, our defenses come down. It is not an interchange of one sword for another, but the first click in the lock to the heretofore barred door that leads to the very heart of the castle of our lives. When that exchange is made, closeness is born.

Although we all hunger for this closeness, many of us are paralyzed by the fear of risking the exchange. Little do we realize that the danger is the fear itself. Only those of us who *do* dare to take the risk will ever know what Jesus meant when he said, "Take and eat, this is my body."

A favorite meditation of mine has always been that of Jesus weeping over Jerusalem. Have you ever felt taken for granted? Have you ever experienced that unique pain of *too much* tenderness—of loving someone so very much and having to endure that person's deafness while he or she slides from hurt to misery to absolute heartbreak? Perhaps all of us have at some time wept on our own mountain, high over Jerusalem.

Every Christian knows that Jesus died on the cross atop a hill. To be sure, we know that hill as Calvary–but there are *many* hills upon which lovers die. Reading that passage I often feel that Jesus had already died before he ever climbed Calvary. In a very real way, he died on that hill above his beloved city.

How easy it is for our human mind to enter the mind of Jesus in this setting. Jerusalem was the holy city, the city of endless longing for all devout Jews. How Jesus must have loved her: her tradition, her symbolism, her people. Looking out over the city, he must have entered those streets in his mind, listened to the busy chatter in the marketplace, watched the children playing in the sunlight, and pondered the neighborhood characters living their song. He probably saw the smoke from the magnificent Temple rise to heaven as the sacrifice was offered to his Father. He saw, and he *knew*.

He knew the Temple would be destroyed, and with it, the children in the afternoon light. The women would wail and the men would be crucified. Desperately, he wanted to avoid that; he wanted them all to come to the fount of living water so that they need not die in the harsh desert of their own souls. He wanted them to come to him that their loneliness would be healed.

"How often have I desired to gather your children together as a hen gathers her brood under her wings, and you were not willing!" (Matthew 23:37). Who cannot relate to that? When read with the mind of love, how close we can draw to that heartbroken stranger (all prophets are strangers) agonizing on that hill above the city that would not recognize its own time of deliverance.

The prayer of listening is the prayer of surrender. It is not a mindless "giving up," but a supremely intelligent "giving over" of the powers of the soul unto a loving, beneficent God–a God who says to us through his Son, "Come to me, all you that are weary and are carrying heavy burdens, and I will give you rest" (Matthew 11:28).

To hear, all we need do is listen.

Prayer of Others

I once heard a strange conclusion to a Sunday sermon. The pastor had focused his comments on the importance of saying what we have to say: "How many of us have within us the stuff to make the hearts of others overflow, but we decline to say it. We hide it—often until it is too late."

After making this point, the pastor invited the congregation into a simple exchange. "We are going to stop now for a few moments. Most of you are here with a family member or a friend. All of us are here as brothers and sisters in Christ. So right now I am going to give you a few moments to say something meaningful to someone. Think about it, then if you have something to say, say it."

At first the church was rather quiet—almost tense. Rarely are we asked to do anything personal in church, anything that requires us to take down the barricades or say anything of who we are. In this particular congregation, no one questioned that there was much to be said. What was at issue was the freedom and ability to say it.

At first, only a few whispers could be heard here and there. In a very short time, however, the church was full of the most appropriate church music anyone ever heard: people sharing.

The looks on the faces of the crowd told their own stories. Many eyes were full of tears of joy or looks of astonishment. So clearly they said, "No kidding! I didn't know that! I had no idea you felt that way!"

So often—too often—we presuppose that others know "where we are." We are so sure that others know how much we love them, that we want things to work out for them, that we need them, that we're sorry. But how often those assumptions are false! Others *don't* know, and what's more, *we* don't know how *they* feel either.

When the sharing faded out that morning at church, the community atmosphere had completely changed. It was more open, more real. There was a far different quality of presence—and all because the prayer of the other had been prayed.

Our need for others

The simple truth is, we need one another. This is, of course, a cliché and a truism, but truisms become such precisely because they are true—in such deep ways that we can easily forget how true they are.

We noted earlier that depression has a constant companion: anger. But if the anger is hidden under some protective cloak, how are we to see its real face? How do we get in touch with what or with whom we are angry?

Prayer and praying become essential elements here, especially the prayer of the other. For it is in dialogue, in communication, in trustful sharing with another, that successive layers of blindness are scraped off, thus giving us the courage, power, and vision to see what is going on inside us.

The key element here is "trust," and we will never grasp that element if we don't venture out, risk, become vulnerable and honest. How can we dare do this, however, if others do not prove themselves to be trustworthy? Such a process will unfold only with the prayer of the other.

Atmosphere is an important element of trust. Upon entering a room or encountering a group of people, we can sense the atmosphere, sometimes immediately. The very air of some gatherings breathes hostility and tension. Other rooms or situations convey an essence of safety and gentleness. Some situations cry out, "Cover up! The demon is here and will brutalize you." Others softly coax, "Come out, unfold, all is safe here. There is room to bloom."

Healing happens not so much as the result of a technique or formula, but within an atmosphere of loving communion. Within such an atmosphere we learn that we are okay, that we have something to say that others will find worthwhile. In a trusting, loving atmosphere we learn that we can do things. In fact we become positively creative—and creativity, after all, is simply the freedom to allow the multitude of forms, shapes, colors, and sounds that glide around inside us to emerge and take shape. Those shapes are in us all. What is *not* inside all of us is the freedom to let that creative life blossom. What holds us back? Perhaps we are afraid that our own creative goodness is not there, that it isn't really "good" or creative, or that we will be laughed at.

But then comes someone, a Don Quixote sort of person, who tells us over and over (as in the play, *The Man of la Mancha*), "I know what I see and you are not Aldonza, the woman for hire. You are Dulcinea; you are my lady." In the play, Don Quixote repeats that dignifying statement so often that the lady comes to believe it. And when she believes it, she *actually becomes* the Lady Dulcinea. The man of La Mancha creates such an atmosphere of respect that she becomes whole. She becomes who she is truly meant to be.

But atmosphere is like sunlight: it doesn't happen without the sun. So, too, a healing atmosphere doesn't happen without people. Without Don Quixote, Dulcinea was Aldonza. Without the mirror, there is no reflection.

The prayer of others—which is fed by the prayer of quiet and the prayer of listening—helps us become a mirror to one another. But no mirror can remain clear when shadows are cast upon it. If the shadowing goes on, it is only a matter of time until it becomes completely dark.

There are countless indications that the prayer of others is present and working in our world. Its power is stupendous. In almost every church, or within reach of every church, we can find a prayer group, charismatic or otherwise. These groups are made up of people who strive mightily in the Lord to create an atmosphere of openness and trust. In their midst, we need not be afraid. Their motive is not to find fault or to compete; rather, honesty rules their actions. In such supportive prayer groups, we learn about who we are and how to live.

The youth group in our parish is just such an atmosphere. There are no officers, no dues, no bylaws. The purpose of the group is to learn to be a family. Each week two persons volunteer to organize the next week's meeting, which means they will prepare a short presentation on a relevant topic.

One night the kids started showing up around seven-thirty. They just sat on the grass, talking and singing songs. For everyone who arrived, there was a hearty welcome. That in itself was significant. How many meetings had these kids previously attended where no one even said hello? They were not seen. With the simple gesture of a gracious welcome, a friendly atmosphere imperceptibly but surely began to form, like the glow of a warm fire.

When the two who had volunteered to lead the meeting started talking, they, too, experienced that initial atmosphere of welcome and warmth. No one rang a bell, called the meeting to order, or read the roll call; members simply offered the presenters the same attention and presence they were offered upon arriving.

The two session leaders read the *Desiderata* and spoke a little on the need to like yourself if others are to have a chance of liking you. Then they asked, "Why are you here tonight?" and opened the gathering for individual responses by first responding themselves.

Once again, the atmosphere of warmth and welcome, the attention and presence of the group, and the openness and honesty of the presenters set the atmosphere. In the entire group of some twenty people, there was only one who decided not to share. Even then, that decision was honored without comment. Amazingly, everyone else—from a seventh-grader to the mother of several of the teenagers—answered in the same way. Basically, they were there to meet and be with others, to have others know them, to feel and be close, to learn to trust and not be afraid. In our terminology, we could say that they were there to learn the prayer of others.

Many of the young people in the group had gone to church with one another for five or six years, and had gone to school together even longer. Yet many important things had been left unsaid among them during those years; they had never prayed the prayer of others. They didn't know how. No one had ever taught them—and the atmosphere had never presented itself. They had never met a Don Quixote.

What followed was extremely touching. The young people moved from one to another, imparting their gift of truth. It was hard not to see them as life-giving bees flitting from flower to flower, taking the sweetness from one and giving it to another. Woven throughout this meeting, the presentations, and the interactions, ran a thread of magic, the magic that appears every time true community forms. The magic is about understanding in your heart that *there is a place where I belong, a place that is safe.* More than anything else, it is just a jumping-off point for the prayer of others. Who would have guessed the wonderful gifts these people were to one another? No one would have–until the prayer of the other was prayed.

Destructive behavior, whether it manifests itself in violence, divorce, alcoholism, drug addiction, apathy, depression, vandalism, or pure squandered potential, does not happen when the prayer of others is at work. As long as one is embraced in such prayer and the supporting kinds of prayer that accompany it, there is great hope.

From the prayer of the other, we learn trust, and only with trust are we willing to exchange sword for key. Without trust, we would be fools to do so. Until the exchange is made, each of us hides away in a barricaded fortress where the atmosphere, although it feels safe, is not supportive of life.

The prayer of the other is a prayer of sharing. It is the essence of trust, and the atmosphere that supports it very clearly says, "Bloom! It is safe here."

Prayer of Acceptance

Just as the prayer of listening presupposes a willingness to hear, the prayer of acceptance presupposes a willingness to seek. Scripture tells us that those who seek, and know what they are looking for, shall find. This prayer concerns itself with what one prayer group calls "God-touches."

God-touches are exactly what the word suggests: gentle touches that bring the Divine into our lives. They can and do happen at any time. What we must ask ourselves is how open are we to being touched and how capable are we of accepting such touches. Any experience of beauty is a God-touch, of course, but the greatest God-touches are experiences of loving and being loved.

To be sure, the world is full of deceit and injury. As the *Desiderata* tells us, however, we should also be alive to the love in the world which is "as perennial as the spring." The prayer of acceptance is the prayer of openness to the song of love that is ever being reborn.

Not too long ago I had the good fortune to see *Peter Pan*. Because it is a "child's film," and I was not comfortable going by myself, I finagled several companions to go with me. Gretchen and Eric are nine; Toddy is six; Cara is five. It was my great luck to be seated between Toddy and Cara. Both children, in them-selves, are God-touches—the way they think, their manner of speech, their openness, and their incredible imagination.

At a certain point in the movie, the plot got scary. We didn't know if Peter would be able to get away from Captain Hook. In the tension of that horrifying uncertainty, a tiny voice to my right said, "Can I sit by you?" It was Toddy. *Sit by me?* He al-ready was. How close can you get? Well, closer than he was, apparently.

Faster than Tinkerbell, Toddy scurried up onto my lap and pulled my right hand around him. Maybe if he felt safer, Peter Pan would be safer too.

It didn't take long before Cara had the same idea. Being afraid for her flying hero, she felt afraid for herself. Pixie that she is, she effortlessly climbed aboard the left side of my lap—and there we sat for the remainder of the movie, each child's head resting on a shoulder. From that moment on, my mind was far from *Peter Pan*.

Perhaps some of you have heard the haunting, moving song from Isaiah where Yahweh proclaims that he will bear us up on eagles' wings and hold us in the palm of his hand. The song promises that there, in the palm of his hand, we will find shelter; there we will be whole. But it is one thing to know the melody and words of the song, and quite another to enter into the emotional content of what the song proclaims. That afternoon the absolutely trustful attitudes of those two little God-touches—in their request and willingness to draw close—seemed to be what that song is about.

If only we adults had such attitudes, we, too, could draw close to the God who would be delighted to hold us close—anywhere we wanted to sit: in his hand, lap, or heart. There is very little in my remembered experience that gives me such a spiritual boost as that velvety soft voice whispering, "Can I sit by you?" even while the little guy was already moving into safety—so sure was he of the answering response.

"Oh, he!"

We aren't likely to find or accept what we do not seek. And we clearly can't "find" if we don't know where or what to seek. How curious that our nature desperately longs for God-touches, that we don't know where to look for these precious touches, and that they are so plentiful!

Moses knew a lot about God-touches. Without getting too academic, it is fascinating to note that scholars say the name God gave himself through the burning bush was not a name at all. The name that Moses brought back to the people was *Yahweh*, not a personal name like John or Mary.

Dr. Martin Buber, the brilliant Jewish scholar, speculated that what Moses heard was a primal expression of an overwhelming presence. According to Dr. Buber, Moses probably heard something like the utterance, "Oh, he!" (Remember, Moses was overwhelmed by what was happening. How would *you* react to a God manifesting himself through a bush that burned, but was not consumed?)

"*Oh, he*"? What in the world does that mean?

Have you every visited a maternity ward and observed the faces and heard the sounds? It's primal noise, primal communication of sound. Even before a name is given to that precious newborn, the "ohhhh…" of a father and mother can be heard as they see their child for the first time, perhaps at the moment of birth itself. About all they can say—which is everything—is "Oh, look, look, look, who it is! The one we've been waiting for is here." This is much like Moses is thought to have spoken.

Some words are strictly functional. Whether they are used to describe, question, or clarify, the crux of the discussion is an object or a defined issue. We can look at it, inspect it, analyze it, perhaps touch it. We "do" unto it.

There are also ecstasy words. These words emerge when what is spoken of is not studied, but entered into. At moments when ecstasy words are used, there are no attempts to describe, analyze, or question. The only response is to accept, surrender, and utter some such primal sound as "Oh, he."

These deepest of God-touches are as true of death as they are of birth. Grief and wailing are primal sounds. They name without specifying. Several times in the past few years, I have heard such wailing. I have heard it from wives who have suddenly and violently lost their husbands, from families who have lost a child.

There are no real words in these utterances, no names—only primal expressions of immense experience that address the situation far better than any descriptive words can. These sounds are not aimed at *describing* the experience–they *are* the experience in the form of sound.

The people who grieve have *lived* with their now-deceased loved one. They shared their lives with them, became part of them. They were not *object* to one another, but *subject*. One of them could not be touched without the other being affected, for in all truth they were not totally separate. As a widow once said to me, "Part of me died with him. It will never live again."

Perhaps there is no better word to indicate the breadth and depth of this love than "temple." For a genuine lover, the other person becomes a true temple of God, a burning bush, a "place" from which the presence of God invites and gives. As we think about it, all of us have heard such primal sounds, these noises that precede the names by which we objectify our experiences. A mother holding her infant, the father at the casket of his drowned son, a man and woman who have fought their way through all the obstacles of trust and have finally arrived in each other's presence: these are all moments when being known is far more important than posturing or denial. At such God-touch moments, we better understand Dr. Buber's supposition that what escaped the heart and lips of Moses was not a word-name, but a primal sound indicating Moses' overwhelming experience of God's presence.

God-touches come in many forms. Some, such as the climbing aboard of Toddy and Cara, can teach much, but do not necessarily descend to the primal level of experience. It is not that God cannot be found there or that the prayer of acceptance cannot be prayed at that moment. But that may not be the *deepest* level at which we can find God.

Deeper levels can be frightening, however. We humans are

very reluctant to be out of control or to surrender to an experience greater than ourselves. So we shy away from them. When we can't avoid such moments, we tend not to replay them. We refuse to reflect on them, and so we never learn what we could from them. The fact is, God can touch us in both joy and pain. Our task is to be open to whatever way this touch comes.

If we are too afraid of being out of control or of being captured by that which is greater than ourselves, we will miss out on the experience. We cannot look upon the face of God and be in control.

Prayer of Ministry

Although the prayer of ministry is characterized by action, all action is not ministry. Contrary to popular belief, the prayer of ministry is not what we give or what we do; rather, the prayer of ministry is what we receive in the giving. It is made possible by the awareness that there is inevitably more to be gained from active ministry to and with others than can ever be given or taught.

Have you ever looked into the face of one of those rare people who is absolutely candid? It is hard to explain this startling experience, but in some marvelous way these few, gift-giving individuals are transparent. Not that we can literally see through them, of course, but when we look into their eyes, we seem to be looking into very clear, deep water.

What's the nature of our inability to plumb that depth? Perhaps it has not so much to do with the clarity of the water as it does with our inability to see. Conversely, what do we see when we look into the face of someone who lacks candor? A wall, to be sure, but what is the wall that blocks transparency?

I suggest that transparency emerges because there is nothing to hide. When there is nothing to hide, there is nothing to forbid another from coming in as guest in that spirit. I'm not suggesting dangerous vulnerability. On the contrary, vulnerability arises from fear that what is hidden might be discovered. In a transparent person, the locked doors have been pried open, and the haunted house has been "de-demonized." Fear and anger have already been faced, and thus are no longer obstacles.

The opposite is true of those who are not transparent at all. The "wall" is made up of unfaced, undealt-with character defects. The building blocks are fear, anger, jealousy, insecurity—all the heavy burdens that clog the spiritual ventilation of the soul. These obstacles not only prevent anyone from seeing or coming in but also (and this is proportionately true) keep *us* from seeing into anyone else. We can lead no one where we ourselves have not gone.

Saints, of course, are the ones who most clearly exemplify that marvelous and rare condition of transparency. They are like the Master; having persevered in their way of life long enough, their way has become their life—not a part of it. They are the ones who have made a total exchange of what needed to die in them so that what groaned to be born could emerge from the womb of life.

There is no other way but the exchange; we cannot have both. The other side of the river cannot be gained without risking the swift current. There can be no freedom from fear unless we face it, and no purity of communication without the risk of dialogue. Those who would escape the slavery of chronic anger—in any of its manifestations, from rage to depression—cannot find serenity without naming that anger. And so it goes; transparency is the mellow state of having nothing to hide.

The cost of holiness

Saint can be a confusing word, of course. Few of us would consider ourselves saints or even aspire to that "status." Start talking about the saints, as a matter of fact, and the clicking sound of turnoffs becomes deafening. Although we can't all be "storybook saints," however, we need not cheat ourselves of the transparency and peace that could be ours.

Saintliness is a matter of degree. A Saint Joseph or a Saint Thérèsa might have been gifted enough to earn transparency to an amazing degree. But that doesn't mean we can have none of it. In fact, the holiness of Joseph and Thérèsa might well mean that we can have as much of "it" as we are willing to pay for.

Pay what? What does it cost? If it is true—and the various kinds of praying suggested here will give you a pretty good idea if it is true for you—that this inner peace comes from the conquest of anger, fear, and hostility, then the main road to both sainthood and free human living is the same. Out-of-control character defects are incompatible with holiness for the same reason they are contrary to human happiness: they block out God and bottle up creative energy. Deep transparency is the mark not only of the saint but also of the successful human being. That, then, is the price of freedom: the willingness to put away games and destructive living for the sake of transparency.

Perhaps some concrete examples will both clarify the point and indicate the necessity of the prayer of ministry.

As strange as it may sound to those whose ears are not used to hearing it, peace, transparency, and successful living require that we recognize the gift that we are in others' lives. We must accept the truth that others need us—and also, of course, that we need them. But how are we ever to learn this and integrate it into our lives? We can't—not if we are not involved in giving to others that we might receive. We simply cannot have if we do not give.

We are all very sure about what others have to give, but we're not always so sure about the gift we are to others. Anger and blocked transparency often turn us into loners. We claim we need no one. In our own minds, strength means going it alone, so we go it alone and experience ourselves as "strong" in the process. We insist that it is the stronger, more noble, and holier person who can give and not receive.

Where do we learn to receive gracefully? Let us return to the swimming party. Those who "gift" us are the ones who show by their brokenness what it means to pass from death to life. They are the ones who heal us. The people we help heal are those we allow to see our need.

The residents of the institute could not change into or out of their suits; they could not move to the pool's edge by them-selves; they could not get into or out of the water alone. In fact, very few could be in the water alone without drowning. But among them there is no such thing as a loner; that is a game they simply don't have the luxury of playing. Rather, in all of them there is a graciousness in accepting the help that is offered. They are consummate teachers in the rare art of joyfully receiving. They show neither resentment of their need to receive nor any kind of pseudo-worship for those who help them. To them, there is simply a reality that must be dealt with. It states, "Look, I want to play in the water. Since I can't do it alone, I will rely on you to help me, and we'll both have a lot of fun." Simple—in the profound way that transparency is simple, in the way that God is simple.

How easily and pervasively the "loner syndrome" seeps into our lives! When we are hurt, in need, angry—or even joyful—we are so often tempted to hide it, "go it alone," we say. "I can weather the storm by myself." Only when the storm passes are we willing to tell another, "Hey, know what happened to me?" But by then it's too late to share the gift of our weakness and neediness. The opportunity has passed. So often we say we want someone "to be there" for us. Yet, do we tell that to others? Do we actually provide others the privilege of "being there" for us?

It isn't easy, this transparent way of life. It hurts to have to work against the feeling that we are not worth anything. It feels very risky to give up the loner attitude for a hoped-for life "with" someone. The alternative, however, is hardly pain-free. As difficult as it is to creep from behind some protective wall, it is even harder to stay behind it. The only alternative is to accept and live with the feeling of worthlessness. There is no free or easy way. Both hurt.

This is not to say that change happens all at once. Remember the marathon runner: one step at a time. The most important step in a thousand-mile journey is the first one. For most of us, progress is a matter of creeping. Seldom are we set free of some slavery "all of a sudden." What sometimes looks like a sudden change is the result of many, many decisions, each one made slowly, one after the other, until it becomes possible to "all of a sudden" step forth. Beginning is what counts: taking that first hesitant step in the belief that one step will lead to another, and then another, until the freedom of transparency is finally found.

The inability to accept limitations or to live up to our own splendid potential is one of the main reasons for a lack of transparency. But not one of us lives without limitations, and very few of us live up to our full potential. Our task is to find and accept both.

There are limitations, of course, that simply have to do with being a human being—the most significant of those human limitations being death itself. There also is a limitation woven into the very fabric of loving: the deeper the love, and the greater the desire for union, the more evident it becomes that the closeness can never be close enough. These painful but inevitable limitations must be accepted.

To embark upon the path of prayer also ushers in a very real limitation. Growth is a hunger. To know any growth or freedom is to know that there can never be enough. There is a limit to where we can be tomorrow, and there is a limit to the speed with which depressive living can be left behind.

Here, in the prayer of ministry, we actually learn to joyfully accept those limitations that cannot be changed. Once that acceptance takes place, we can get busy actualizing what we do have instead of bemoaning that which we don't. It is then that we discover, in spite of our limitations, just how rich we truly are.

Mary, the swimming-party guest, cannot walk, speak, hear, hold a comb, or brush her teeth. But she enjoyed the water, felt its coolness, laughed at all the fun around her, and rejoiced in the love of her friend, Frank, who knew to look into her eyes to see what she was saying. Mary can teach us much about giving, receiving, and accepting limitations. Such is the reward of those who engage in the prayer of ministry.

A parable about two bodies of water familiar to Jesus states the case of the prayer of ministry. One body of water is fresh and brims with life. While splashes of green adorn its banks, trees spread their branches over it and stretch out thirsty roots to sip of its healing waters. Along its shores the children play, as children played when Jesus was there. He loved it. He could look across its silver surface when he spoke his own parables.

The river Jordan, sparkling with water from the hills, feeds this body of water called the Sea of Galilee. Man and animal alike build their homes on its banks. Every kind of life is happier because of this life-giving body of water.

The river Jordan flows south into another sea. There is no brimming life near that body of water, no splash of color along the bank, no fluttering leaf, no song of birds, no children's laughter. Unless they are on urgent business, travelers choose another route. The air hangs heavy above this body of water, appropriately called the Dead Sea, and neither man nor beast nor fowl will drink there.

What makes the dramatic difference in these neighboring seas? Certainly not the river Jordan; it empties the same good water into both. Certainly not the soil in which both seas lie. Certainly not the surrounding countryside.

The difference is this: the Sea of Galilee receives but does not keep the waters of the Jordan. For every drop that flows into it, another drop flows out. The Dead Sea, on the other hand, is shrewd, hoarding its income jealously. Every drop it receives, it keeps. The Sea of Galilee gives and lives; the Dead Sea gives nothing, and is "dead."

"Are We Ready…?"

Recall the questions that opened this chapter: "Are we ready to stop defining ourselves by our brokenness? Are we willing to walk with this God who has revealed himself in the whispering breeze, in the crops ripe for the harvest, and in his Son, Jesus, who has come to walk with us?"

Are we?

I believe the greatest courage of all is not some brief flash of heroism, but rather in the commitment to simply not give up. The greatest courage is to get up every day, embrace the day with the cards at hand, and make the best of what God has given us. The edge, however–the edge gamblers, warriors, generals, and risktakers are always looking for, the edge we have–is that there is a Power, ever near, not of this earth. The promise God made us through Jesus to always be with us, to care for us to the extent that "the very hairs of your head are numbered" is real. Jesus was not into hype. He spoke literal truth.

As we are called every day to exhibit that greatest of all courage, to just show up, step up to the plate and take our swings, let us do so with the unswerving confidence that we do not step up alone. That is the edge. There the Power is deeper than any darkness, higher than any fear, stronger than the strongest pull of fear, doubt, guilt, or past failures. We do not ride forward alone. If this book, with all it's exercises, tools, triangles, and text, says anything, let it be this above all: we do not go alone. As we daily take up the challenge to charge the darkness, we do not go alone.

> Lord, help me to strive daily to be a more loving, concerned, and sharing person. It is in giving that I, too, will receive. For by enriching the lives of others, I find my own greatest fulfillment. If I am willing to surrender the false ego–the little self–and lose myself in a dream, a goal, an ambition, in love and service to others, then, and only then, will I experience a foretaste of heaven.

Afterword

A woman in Texas wrote, "Lately, a lot of problems have kept me depressed, worried, and in great fear of getting older. I feel a great need to hurry. But also, I just want to sit down and quit. I wish life would hurry up and get over with. I don't understand how to deal with those feelings. I want to do things right, but I feel lost. I feel there is a piece missing—an important piece. I have no one to turn to. Professional help is too expensive. What you were talking about in your books made me think maybe you have the part I am missing. Please help me to understand what is happening to my life."

There are many themes in these few words that, when weaved together, become the tattered coat of DLS. Depressing problems, worry, and fear; a sincere desire to do what is right; feeling there is a missing piece; and the pressing sense of being alone with it all: this is the reality of DLS.

Because I didn't now this woman personally, I could answer in only the most general of terms. I also sent her an early draft of this book. It's what I know about DLS. From the deepest part of my heart, I urged her to make a call to a Twelve Step group, where she could be referred to a self-help community in her area that would offer acceptance and love. They do exist, I told her; love is available.

Since the woman made no mention of her relationship with God as she understood God to be, I didn't know what to tell her about faith. Rather than risk assumptions, I told her this story about my grandsons. I threw this story into the pond of her life, having no idea what kind of ripples it would create—if any. But I don't have to know the results; that is between her and God. My job is simply to throw the stone into the pond to the best of my ability; God does the rest. I share the story with you as well; it truly touched my heart.

Two of the most brilliant sources of God's light in my life are my grandsons. They are angels in the biblical sense: messengers of God's presence. Montgomery is four; Loren is two.

Last year, my wife and I took our grandsons to the state fair. Among the attractions was a huge playhouse with a long slide, perhaps thirty feet long. Montgomery was feeling his oats and decided he wanted to go down the long slide—quite a distance for a small boy. "You come with me, Grandpa," he insisted. Like picking up after the elephants, I wanted to do that slide. I wasn't even sure I'd fit. But how do you say "no" to an angel?

Up into the playhouse we went, picking our way to the top of the slide. After the first few steps, Montgomery began to feel fear. Again and again I encouraged him, "I'm right here, Buddy. No problem. We can do this." Up ladders, over small obstacles, through tunnels; up, always up. When we came to a particularly scary bridge made of shaky boards, Montgomery stopped. He was afraid to tempt the swaying bridge.

"I'm right beside you. Come on, take my hand. I'm right here. Let's get over this sucker." At that point, I knew it would be ten times harder to go back down than forward, so we went on. With enough encouragement, coupled with constant touch, Montgomery got to the summit. Like tackling Mount Everest, we stood there atop of the slide, somehow victorious.

Still shaky, but with my encouragement, my pint-sized angel situated himself on the slide and sailed downward, leaving me to try to fit myself into the chute. Actually, the ride down wasn't half bad.

"Ah," you say, "the point is clear." Not yet.

Loren decided it was time for him to get some attention, so as soon as my feet hit the ground, he wanted to go to the petting zoo—so off we went.

In the meantime, Montgomery was feeling pretty confident. He decided that he didn't need any help negotiating the obstacles up the slide, so off he went on his own. But when he once again came to the bridge, he stopped. His fear won out over his courage. All he could do was sit there before the obstacle and cry, like the woman from Texas: "I just want to sit down and quit." It took a wise attendant to climb the slide, cross the bridge with Montgomery, and encourage him the rest of the way. When I returned, Montgomery turned his tear-stained eyes up to me and said, "Grandpa, I got scared. Where were you?"

There's the point: no one does it alone. No one needs to do it alone. We all have our frightening bridges that we simply cannot cross alone. What is no big deal for one might be a major feat for another. What the bridge *is* makes no different. The fact that there is a shaky bridge, or two, in our life is the point—plus the fact that we can find support and encouragement as we attempt to cross.

For many of us, the shakiest bridge of all is asking for help. Going it alone doesn't take all that much courage for alone, we can close up like a clam. It is risking our deepest selves, reaching out a hand, making a call, writing a letter, saying a prayer; this is courage. Dying is easy; it's living that is hard.

With my story about Montgomery, I urged the woman from Texas to trust, to reach out, to open up. Even if the best she can do right now is a faltering, stumbling half step, take it.

I can guarantee you this: just as there is nothing I would deny my two angels that is for their good, there is a heavenly Father who will deny you nothing. If I was faithful in my support, guidance, encouragement, and protection of my grandson, imagine the passion of an all-loving God going behind you, before you, alongside you—whatever direction you want. God is there pushing you from behind, calling you from in front, encouraging you alongside. All you have to do is listen—listen and say, "Yes."

Walk well with those who love you and with God who loves you perfectly, unconditionally, limitlessly.

Index

About the Authors

E arnie Larsen is the author of more than forty books on topics ranging from self-help to spirituality. For over thirty years, Earnie has been minister, counselor, seminar presenter, and friend to hundreds of thousands of people trying to make their way, as best they can, through the difficult and dangerous parts of life.

In the early eighties, Earnie Larsen founded E. Larsen Enterprises, a corporation that promotes personal growth and recovery. For product information or for a product brochure call 1-800-635-4780 (FAX: 612-560-9627) or write E. Larsen Enterprises, Inc., 5820 74th Avenue North, #106, Brooklyn Park, MN 55443.

Cara A. Macken, M.S., CHES, is director of the Comprehensive School Health Education Program for the state of South Dakota. She is committed to health issues, especially as they apply to women.